ENDORSEM

Running by Faith is a compelling book of relatable life experiences with Bible verses to support challenges we may face in our lives. It's refreshing to know it is offered as a guide to inspire, motivate, and encourage people to live boldly and courageously for our Lord and Savior, and to have the confidence to know that we can always depend on Him. My husband, Autry, has shared his experience and wisdom wholeheartedly, which is why this book would be a great complement to anyone's journey to become more like Christ.

Elaine N. Denson

wife and best friend

What an awesome God we serve that He saw it fit to preserve my friendship with Autry for over thirty years! Proverbs 18:24 reads, "One who has unreliable friends soon comes to ruin, but there is a friend who sticks closer than a brother."

I am blessed that we chose the latter and we "stuck" closer to each other like brothers. For the record, it was not easy, but it definitely has been worth it, as Autry and I have been able to live out our dreams together with our families.

Running by Faith will definitely bless you! It demonstrates the power of obedience and how one young man from Lauderhill, Florida, can make a difference in countless people's lives as he allows God to work through him. I find it the utmost honor to call Autry Lamont Denson, Jr. "a friend who sticks closer than a brother."

Marlon L. Llewellyn

"A friend who sticks closer than a brother."

servant leader and Director of School Development and Leadership at GEO Foundation

Running by Faith is a God-inspired guide to recognizing His will in our daily struggles and circumstances. Autry Denson's candid experiences and transparency make him the perfect vessel to communicate this will. You will certainly enjoy this collection of stories, but more importantly, they will feed your soul.

Min. Cyril G. Guerra, Jr.
Executive Minister–Hopewell Missionary Baptist Church
Pompano Beach, FL–In His Service

Autry has been a beacon of light for me and so many others over the last several years. *Running by Faith* shares twenty-three inspiring and powerful stories that encourage and equip us all with the tools to live sold out and on fire for Christ every day, and to make a lasting impact on the lives of the people we care about most. Autry gives us a motivating set of practical strategies through the word of God and uses the running metaphor like a great coach, encouraging us to use our time, talents, and resources more effectively. Take Autry's applicable strategies to heart to produce more joy, happiness, and success in your life. This is a must-read if you want to be lifted up and strengthened with applicable lessons to help fulfill your purpose in life.

Chuck Pagano
veteran NFL coach and former Head Coach–Indianapolis Colts

RUNNING BY FAITH

2-Minute Devotionals with Eternal Impact

Autry L. Denson, Jr.

Denson Family Legacy Publishing, LLC

Summerville, SC 29486

Running by Faith
Two-Minute Devotionals with Eternal Impact

Autry L. Denson, Jr.
Denson Family Legacy Publishing

Published by Denson Family Legacy Publishing, Summerville, South Carolina
Copyright ©2021 Autry L. Denson, Jr.
All rights reserved.

Project Management and Book Design:
    Davis Creative Publishing Partners, DavisCreative.com

Editor: Elaine N. Denson

Library of Congress Cataloging-in-Publication Data
Library of Congress Control Number: 2021908639
Autry L. Denson, Jr.
Running by Faith: Two-Minute Devotionals with Eternal Impact
ISBN: 978-1-7371357-0-8 (paperback)
        978-1-7371357-1-5 (ebook)

BISAC subject headings:

  1.   REL108030 RELIGION / Christian Living / Leadership & Mentoring
       2. REL012040 RELIGION / Christian Living / Inspirational   3. YAN048020
       YOUNG ADULT NONFICTION / Religious / Christian / Devotional & Prayer

2021

ACKNOWLEDGMENTS

I would like to thank my Lord and Savior Jesus Christ who placed it on my heart to write this book. My parents, Janice and Leroy Franklin, and my father, Autry Denson, Sr., for instilling in me and my sisters the importance of having a strong spiritual foundation. As a result, nothing is more important than my relationship with God. My two sisters, Tanisha and Natasha, who have always had my back since I was a little dude running around our street on 46th Avenue in Lauderhill, Florida. Next, I would like to thank my beautiful wife Elaine for her love, support, and willingness to offer honest critique, as well as always being a sounding board upon which I can share the many things God places on my heart. It has been over twenty years that I have been rocking with you, and I can honestly say that every day gets sweeter and sweeter, my dear. My children—and when I say "children," I am talking about my crew—Ashley, Autry, Elijah, and Asia, as well as Tiffany, Tyra, TJ, Dre, Paige, Taylor, Terrence, Little Byron, Xzavier, and Carter. And my grandchildren, Ace and Aubrey. I love y'all so much. It is an honor to watch each of you grow and mature into the young men and women God has created y'all to be. My prayer is that by God's grace, the best is yet to come. Truth be told, y'all are the original "running by faith" crew. I have been applying these lessons since y'all have been born, trying my best not to mess y'all up too badly (smile). My high school head coach, Willie Dodaro, his lovely wife Janette, and their two beautiful daughters, Maria and Tara. Thank you so much for being so unselfish and supportive all the years Coach D has been a high school coach. That time has been well spent turning boys like me into the men God created us to be. Coach Desmond Robinson, his wife Pearl, and his children, Jason and Ashley—the same goes for you all. Coach Rob was the first coach I ever had who did not curse, and boldly lived his faith out loud and on purpose for everyone to see. It has been almost twenty years, and I am still reaping the benefits from his godly example. Like him, I, too, preached my first sermon while I was a football coach at the University of Notre Dame. To my boy, Scott Booker, and to Jen and Morgan—man, y'all are family. I am so blessed to have gotten the chance to know "Book," and in case y'all didn't know, y'all are stuck with the Denson Crew! Last but not least, to my brother from another mother, Marlon Llewellyn, his mother, the late Carol Loftman (more affectionately known as "Mommy"), his wife Tracy, son Bryce (Skip), and daughter Emerson (Cakes). Marlon, you tell me what is impossible with God: Nothing! Jesus said in Luke 18:27, "The things which are impossible with men are possible with God." My brother, we started off on this journey together over thirty years ago and God has kept us joined at the hip ever since. Together, we moved thousands of miles from home to go to college in the same state, graduated and moved back home together, and got jobs that took us all over the country. But we serve a God who not only hears prayers, but answers them. What people don't understand is that we are not lucky. What we are is prayerful. It all started at a basketball court and a youth football field where we made a pact bonded in prayer that if God blessed us to use sports to get a scholarship to attend college, that through prayer and constant support of one another, nothing would stop us from achieving our goals. Goals of graduating, which put a smile on both of our mothers' faces; goals of striving to be godly husbands and fathers when the time presented itself; and goals of loving each other enough to always tell the other what we *need* to hear and never just what we *want* to hear. Over the years, we have laughed together, experienced heartache together, witnessed the births of each other's children, gotten married, literally, a week apart, and now, by God's grace, we get to experience the fruition of this devotional together. In fact, it was you, big bro, who held me accountable and made sure I was writing daily. And you actually came up with the name of this book, *Running by Faith*, which is so fitting because when I look back over our lives, that is exactly what we have been doing. If it's the Lord's will, I pray we will run on for another thirty years, my brother. To all my former teammates from Lauderhill, Nova, Notre Dame, the NFL, my former teachers, neighbors on 46th Avenue, and all those who ever took the time out to sow into my life, I sincerely thank, love, and appreciate you. I am nothing more than a product of God's grace and mercy poured out through loving people like all of you. In return, my commitment is that as long as God wakes me up each morning, I am determined to continue *running by faith*! I love y'all. God bless.

TABLE OF CONTENTS

ACKNOWLEDGMENTS V

TURABIAN STYLE FORMAT 1

INTRODUCTION 3

DAY 23 – YOUR WORD IS YOUR BOND 5

DAY 22 – WARNING! 8

DAY 21 – THE GOOD LIFE 11

DAY 20 – THE GOLDEN RULE 15

DAY 19 – THE DEAL OF A LIFETIME: FAITHFUL TITHING 18

DAY 18 – RESET 21

DAY 17 – RANDOM ACTS OF KINDNESS 25

DAY 16 – LET'S TALK ABOUT SEX 28

DAY 15 – INTOXICATED 35

DAY 14 – IN DUE TIME 39

DAY 13 – I CHOOSE LOVE 42

THE MOVEMENT — WE CHOOSE LOVE 45

DAY 12 – EVERYDAY HEROES OF FAITH 47

DAY 11 – HEADPHONES AND SMARTPHONES:
THE CURRENT DOORWAYS TO SECRET SINS 53

DAY 10 – GREATNESS: GHEA –
GOD HONORING EFFORT AND ATTITUDE 56

DAY 9 – FOR THE LOVE OF MONEY 59

DAY 8 – DISTRACTIONS 62

DAY 7 – DEBT 67

DAY 6 – DEALING WITH ANXIETY 72

DAY 5 – CONTENT, NOT COMPLACENT 77

DAY 4 – CALLED TO LIVE A COUNTERCULTURAL LIFE 81

DAY 3 – BE MINDFUL OF THE COMPANY YOU KEEP 85

DAY 2 – AN UNEXPECTED END 91

DAY 1 – THE BEGINNING 97

FROM THE AUTHOR 99

ABOUT THIS BOOK 100

BIBLE VERSE INDEX 101

BIBLIOGRAPHY 121

ABOUT THE AUTHOR..123

TURABIAN STYLE FORMAT

I have chosen to use the Turabian style format throughout this devotional. If you are like me and enjoy taking notes as you read along but do not like having to search throughout the book for the meanings of words or phrases, this format will make the information accessible through footnotes and endnotes within that day's devotional that you are reading. Since these are designed to be short, two-minute devotionals, and time is of the essence, this will allow you to invest more of your time examining what you are reading for ways to apply this content in your life. In addition, Turabian style formatting still contains the standard bibliography that appears at the back of the book. Once you are done reading and would like to learn more about specific resources and content within the devotional, you can do so by referencing the bibliography. Turabian style formatting gives you the best of both worlds by providing less interrupted reading with comprehension, while also allowing future follow-up, research, and references.

INTRODUCTION

God placed this book on my heart for the purpose of bringing His unchanging, infallible word to the ever-changing circumstances of our daily lives. If you look around, there are so many hurt people who, in turn, are perpetuating the cycle of hurt by hurting other people. About a year ago, I got to the point where my heart couldn't take it anymore. As a result of God's discernment and direction, I was called into action to present the word of God in a manner that is focused on providing application. That's when *Running by Faith* was born. It is a collection of twenty-three short, two-minute devotional stories. Each devotion is accompanied by a section called "Let's Talk About It," which is designed to promote personal reflection and to serve as the catalyst for healthy group discussions. There is also a section called "Go Tell That," which are Bible scriptures that I encourage you to commit to memory, as well as share with others. In addition, the structure of the book is arranged with the chapters in descending order. This represents the countercultural mindset we must have as Christians—to stop looking out to the world for answers to the many situations we face in our daily lives, but instead, to look to the word of God.

The significance of the number "23" is that it is a chapter in the book of Psalms that represents the Lord as my faithful shepherd who has been leading, protecting, and ordering the steps of my life. Twenty-three was also the jersey number I wore as a running back in high school, college, and as a member of the National Football League with the Tampa Bay Buccaneers. As I look back over my life, I am reminded of how God has blessed me with so many life experiences through sports, and in particular the game of football, to use as a platform for ministry. My current position as a college football head coach is further evidence that this has been God's plan, as my shepherd, all along. My prayer is that after you read this devotional, you will be encouraged to use your daily, God-ordained platforms to run this race we call life by faith in God's good and perfect plan. So, get ready – set – let's go!

DAY 23
YOUR WORD IS YOUR BOND

All you need to say is simply 'Yes' or 'No';
anything beyond this comes from the evil one.
Matthew 5:37 (NIV)

There used to be a time when business deals were done by word of mouth. The reason this was possible is because people's primary goal in life was to live in a manner that provided a track record of impeccable character, of honoring their commitments. As a result, their word would be esteemed as having very high value. There was no need for a formal contract because they were engaged in a covenant. The difference between a contract and a covenant lies in the underlying intent. A contract is formed out of distrust and is put in place for protection when something goes wrong. A covenant, on the other hand, is a mutual agreement that brings about a relationship of commitment between two parties. I am by no means saying that there is no place in our lives for contracts, but I am advocating that we filter our intentions, which definitely include our words, through the word of God, and then respond to what it says. Because, contrary to what our current culture may suggest, God's word was relevant back then and is still very relevant right now. So, instead of all the empty promises and pledges, as Christians, according to Matthew 5:37, "All you need to say is simply 'Yes' or 'No'; anything beyond this comes from the evil one" (NIV).

In order for this to happen, it means we have to be committed to making sure that our actions align with our words—not some of the time, not most of the time, but *all* of the time. There is a quote that says, "God gave us one mouth and two ears so we can listen twice as much as we speak." This statement stresses the importance of us valuing the words we choose to speak through mastering the practice of learning to listen, not for the purpose of responding, but for the benefit of understanding. As a result, instead of us speaking words hastily or irresponsibly that may damage our character, we can speak boldly and confidently in a manner that is in alignment with our level of commitment. Many times in the Bible this is seen as wisdom. By most accounts, people would consider it the ultimate compliment to be thought of as wise. Well then, wise people do not allow their words to choose them. Instead, they choose their words. As a result, their words become credible, and the need to do anything other than *give* their word becomes unnecessary. As ambassadors on a mission for God, our words do not just need to be our bond; they are our weapons as we fight on behalf of the kingdom of God. It is imperative that we do not lose the power that is found within them by tainting them with broken promises and empty pledges. So, let's be mindful as Christians that when we say we are going to do something, then for the kingdom's sake, we must do it.

LET'S TALK ABOUT IT

1. In what areas of your life are you confident that when you speak, those around you will take your word as being the truth and not require you to jump through hoops to prove that they can believe what you're saying?

2. In what areas of your life do you need to improve so that your actions align with your words?

3. As Christians, we have been given the word of God as a weapon to fight on behalf of the kingdom. How much more important is it that our words not be wasted on broken promises or empty pledges?

GO TELL THAT

Matthew 5:3337 (MSG)

"And don't say anything you don't mean. This counsel is embedded deep in our traditions. You only make things worse when you lay down a smoke screen of pious talk, saying, 'I'll pray for you,' and never doing it, or saying, 'God be with you,' and not meaning it. You don't make your words true by embellishing them with religious lace. In making your speech sound more religious, it becomes less true. Just say 'yes' and 'no.' When you manipulate words to get your own way, you go wrong."

DAY 22
WARNING!

*Therefore we must give the most earnest heed
to the things we have heard, lest we drift away.*
Hebrews 2:1 (NKJV)

W arning signs are designed to keep us away from danger. Physically, our bodies give off warning signs to alert us when they are not working properly so we can adjust what we are doing. In relationships, warning signs let us know when our spouses or friends are in agreement or at odds with us. As we drive our cars, we see signs that direct the flow of traffic to prevent accidents from occurring. Likewise, spiritual warning signs alert us that we are moving in the wrong direction. This happens when we drift away from God and end up outside of His will. If we do not turn back to Him, an accident is inevitable. However, all warning signs are only effective if we pay attention to them. Let's spend a few minutes examining Hebrews 2:1 to see how we can stay the course for Christ or get back on course if, in the midst of doing life, we have gotten off track. The verse says, "Therefore we must give the most earnest heed to things we have heard, lest we drift away" (NKJV).

Give the most earnest heed

means to diligently apply one's mind and pay detailed attention to the message of Christ. Simply put, the message of Christ is of Jesus' death on the cross and resurrection to restore us into relationship with God.

Things we have heard

refers to four ways we are able to hear and receive the word of God. The first way is by spending time alone with Christ reading His word so we can get to know Him better. The second is by attending church so we can hear the word of God preached. The next way we hear the word of God is by engaging Him in conversation through prayer. Finally, we hear by faithfully and patiently waiting for a response to our prayers.

Lest we drift away

uses nautical terms to urge us to take the things we have heard in regard to the teachings of Christ seriously, for risk of drifting away from the truth of God's word. Author D.A. Carson speaks about the dangers of drifting when he says,

> "We drift toward compromise and call it tolerance; we drift toward disobedience and call it freedom; we drift toward superstition and call it faith. We cherish the indiscipline of lost self-control and call it relaxation; we slouch toward prayerlessness and delude ourselves into thinking we have escaped legalism; we slide toward godlessness and convince ourselves we have been liberated."[1]

Let's be mindful to take heed to the spiritual warning signs in our lives, and to be courageous enough to sound the alarm on behalf of our brothers and sisters in Christ, so they, too, may be warned about the dangers of living outside of the will of God.

---

1 Carson, n.d.

LET'S TALK ABOUT IT

1. In the spirit of transparency, in what areas of your life have you been ignoring the warning signs?
2. Since an accident is the inevitable result of ignoring warning signs, what is keeping you from making the necessary changes?
3. When do you feel will be the right time to implement changes? If your answer is "not today," then when?

GO TELL THAT

1 Peter 3:18 (NIV)

For Christ also suffered once for sins, the righteous for the unrighteous, to bring you to God. He was put to death in the body but made alive in the Spirit.

Romans 10:17 (NIV)

Consequently, faith comes from hearing the message, and the message is heard through the word about Christ.

Hebrews 10:25 (NIV)

Not giving up meeting together, as some are in the habit of doing, but encouraging one another—and all the more as you see the Day approaching.

1 Timothy 4:16 (NIV)

Watch your life and doctrine closely. Persevere in them, because if you do, you will save both yourself and your hearers.

DAY 21
THE GOOD LIFE

And what do you benefit if you gain the whole world but lose your own soul?
Mark 8:36 (NLT)

King Solomon was known as the wisest king to ever live. It's been recorded in the Bible that God blessed him with wisdom, riches[2], land, peace during his reign, and if that were not enough, God would have given him more. More? What *more* is there? It sounds like God already hooked Solomon up with everything he could ever want or need! I'm sure we all would be more than happy if God blessed us with half of that, or better yet, just a fraction of that. However, in spite of accumulating more worldly possessions than anyone else to ever walk the face of the earth, Solomon admits that none of this matters if your priorities in life are out of whack. In Ecclesiastes 1:2-3 he says, "'Everything is meaningless,' says the Teacher, 'completely meaningless!' What do people get for all their hard work under the sun?" (NLT).

To further prove his point, the wisest and richest king to ever live wrote the entire book of Ecclesiastes as a personal reflection of a life lived by a man who regretted wasting time in the pursuit of frivolous stuff—such as sex, money, power, position, and prestige—only to get to the end of his life to realize that the only things that last are what you do for the kingdom of God. Now, I know exactly what you're

---

2   There are four primary ways King Solomon, in a fairly short period of time, became the wealthiest king alive. He was made rich through commerce and trading, gifts he received, tribute money paid to him, and heavy taxation.

thinking because I used to think the same thing. How bad could it be to live a life like Solomon with access to anything your heart desires? After all, isn't that what the world would categorize as the "good life?" Well, unfortunately, the final narrative of Solomon's life speaks—no, actually, it is *shouting out* to all of us, and any of us who will listen, to stop wasting our time in the pursuit of more to achieve the proverbial "good life." Instead, we should live our lives on a mission for and with a good God[3].

So, what do both of these look like? Let's start with the world's definition of the "good life," which is, in essence, the relentless pursuit and acquisition of more—More money, more stuff, more sex, more access, more notoriety. I mean, the list goes on and on. The primary issue with the world's definition of the "good life" is that it is perpetual. There is no end game because it never ends, and enough will never be enough. As human beings, we all have tolerance levels, both good and bad, that must be fed according to the appetites of our desires. The tolerance level demanded by the appetite of the world's "good life" is insatiable. That means it is impossible to satisfy because it is unquenchable, unappeasable, and uncontrollable.

However, the biblical definition of the "good life" is being on mission with and for a good God. We view each day as a blessing from God to be used for His purpose and will to be done. As a result, the end game is simple: to live according to the Great Commandment, which gives us the courage to live out the Great Commission. As hip-hop gospel artist and pastor Trip Lee says, "The good life on mission with and for our good God is the life that has been laid down."[4] Today is a great day to lay down *your* will so you can be alive and available

---

3 Only God is good. Luke 18:19

4 Lee 2012

to be used for your *heavenly Father's* will. So, will you continue to run on the perpetual hamster wheel in pursuit of what the world says the "good life" is, or will you choose to be bold enough to get off and live the "good life" set forth and outlined within the Good Book?

LET'S TALK ABOUT IT

1. What is your definition of the "good life?"
2. Is your definition of the "good life" a result of what others have defined for you as being good or that has been outlined within the Good Book?
3. There is a saying that "When you know better, then you do better." How does knowing what the Good Book defines as the "good life" determine how you live your current life?

GO TELL THAT

2 Corinthians 4:18 (NIV)

So we fix our eyes not on what is seen, but on what is unseen, since what is seen is temporary, but what is unseen is eternal.

Matthew 22:36-40 (NIV)

"Teacher, which is the greatest commandment in the Law?"
Jesus replied: "'Love the Lord your God with all your heart and with all your soul and with all your mind.' This is the first and greatest commandment. And the second is like it: 'Love your neighbor as yourself.' All the Law and the Prophets hang on these two commandments."

Matthew 28:16-20 (NIV)

Then the eleven disciples went to Galilee, to the mountain where Jesus had told them to go. When they saw him, they worshiped him; but some doubted. Then Jesus came to them and said, "All authority in heaven and on earth has been given to me. Therefore go and make disciples of all nations, baptizing them in the name of the Father and of the Son and of the Holy Spirit, and teaching them to obey everything I have commanded you. And surely I am with you always, to the very end of the age."

DAY 20
THE GOLDEN RULE

*Do to others whatever you would like them to do to you. This is the
essence of all that is taught in the law and the prophets.*
Matthew 7:12 (NLT)

I know this may seem like I am stating the obvious. In fact, most
of us have been told this our entire lives by parents, pastors, teachers, coaches, and mentors, to the point where we take it for granted
because we feel like it's just common sense. However, if we look
around at what is going on in society in regard to applying something
as common sense as the Golden Rule *should* be, then it would appear
that common sense is not so common anymore. What, by chance, is
the Golden Rule, you ask? The Golden Rule implies that we should
treat others in the manner that we ourselves want to be treated. It is
very much in alignment with what Jesus Himself considers to be the
second greatest and important commandment to be obeyed. In the
book of Matthew, chapter 22, verses 34-40, the Pharisees questioned
Jesus about which commandment in the law was the greatest. Jesus
responded by stating, "'You shall love the LORD your God with all
your heart, with all your soul, and with all your mind.' This is the first
and great commandment. *And the second is like it: 'You shall love your
neighbor as yourself'*" (emphasis added, NKJV). When talking about
Jesus' statement in HarperCollins' *Bible Dictionary*, the book's general
editor, Paul J. Achtemeier, says, "Furthermore, Jesus used the term in
the English language during the seventeenth century as 'The Golden
Law' for a saying that he regarded as inestimable ("golden") and of

universal importance."[5] The word "inestimable" means "too great to calculate." So, in other words, Jesus held this in such high regard that it's value could not be calculated. I would argue that if Jesus valued this principle, then, as His followers, we should value it also.

We must strive to move past simply knowing what to do to actually doing what Jesus did. We must look for opportunities to practice applying the Golden Rule in our daily lives. My coach when I was little, who also happened to be my dad, used to always say, "Practice does not make perfect, but perfect practice makes perfect." Now, because of God's unconditional love, grace, and mercy, we are not called to be perfect, but we are called to obediently serve God by loving His people. Therefore, we must intentionally practice applying the Golden Rule until it becomes a lifestyle. A lifestyle that enables us to transform interactions that would normally result in conflict and further division into God-honoring interactions that bring us together as one race—the human race—created in God's image, for His glory.

LET'S TALK ABOUT IT

The three Golden Rule questions are designed to break down walls and build bridges that God- honoring relationships, rooted in love, compassion, forgiveness, and reconciliation, can be built upon.

1. Is what I'm about to say or do going to help or hurt the situation?
2. Is the manner in which I am going to say it or do it pleasing to God?
3. Would I appreciate it if it were said or done to me?

---

5 Achtemeier 1996

GO TELL THAT

Luke 6:31 (ESV)

And as you wish that others would do to you, do so to them.

Mark 12:31 (ESV)

"The second is this: 'You shall love your neighbor as yourself.' There is no other commandment greater than these."

DAY 19
THE DEAL OF A LIFETIME: FAITHFUL TITHING

Give, and it will be given to you. A good measure, pressed down, shaken together and running over, will be poured into your lap. For with the measure you use, it will be measured to you.
Luke 6:38 (NIV)

I have a proposition for you. I want you to trust me to provide for all of your needs. That's right, you heard me correctly. But just in case you're in shock, I'll repeat it so that we are clear. The proposition is that I would like to provide for all of your needs. However, there are a few stipulations that will be required. The first stipulation is that of the 100 percent that I give you, I want you to return only 10 percent back to me. The second stipulation is that you be committed to prioritizing the return of my 10 percent first, before you do anything else. The final stipulation is that you do this regularly with a willing heart. Now before you answer, let me sweeten the deal a little more: When you do all these things in the manner that I am requiring you to do them, I will reward you with more because you will have shown that you could be faithful with a little. Is this not a deal of a lifetime? Well, you can call it that or you can call it what God calls it, which is "tithing."

My church in Pompano Beach, Florida, Hopewell Mission-ary Baptist Church, has a saying about tithing that goes like this: "At Hopewell, we do not give to be seen, but we feel everyone should be seen giving." Not only is there a lot of sound wisdom and power in that statement, but within it lies what I have found to be the liberation from the burden of financial worry. I know you are asking, "How can I give my money away and have fewer financial worries?" The answer to the question lies in redefining what faithful tithing really is, as opposed to what the world has so aggressively vilified it to be for the purpose of keeping you in financial bondage.

Faithful tithing is the realization that we are called by God to be good stewards of the material things that He has blessed us with, not the owners. God alone created everything and owns everything. The New Living Translation of Psalm 24:1 says, "The earth is the LORD's, and everything in it. The world and all its people belong to him." Faithful tithing is how we model obedience. News flash: God does not need our tithes, but what He does need from His children is our obedience. Obedience is one of the ways we put our love for God on display before an unbelieving world. Faithful tithing is sacrificial. God has given us everything we have, including sacrificing His own Son on the cross for our sins. Surely, we can make the sacrifice to return back only 10 percent of the 100 percent He has given us, while keeping 90 percent of what He has so graciously blessed us with. Lastly, faithful tithing is what we get the *privilege* to do and not what we *have* to do in order to provide financially for the advancement of the kingdom of God. Therefore, it is evident that faithful tithing is more than the deal of a lifetime. It is actually the deal of eternity.

LET'S TALK ABOUT IT

1. Before reading this devotional, what were your views in regard to tithing?
2. After reading this devotional, have your views about tithing changed? If so, how? If not, why?
3. How does understanding the various reasons for tithing affect how you go about acquiring money, as well as the emphasis you place on who, in fact, is the rightful owner of it?

GO TELL THAT

Genesis 14:19-20 (NIV)

And he blessed Abram, saying,

"Blessed be Abram by God Most High,

Creator of heaven and earth.

And praise be to God Most High,

who delivered your enemies into your hand."

Then Abram gave him a tenth of everything.

Deuteronomy 12:5-6 (NIV)

But you are to seek the place the LORD your God will choose from among all your tribes to put his Name there for his dwelling. To that place you must go; there bring your burnt offerings and sacrifices, your tithes and special gifts, what you have vowed to give and your freewill offerings, and the firstborn of your herds and flocks.

DAY 18
RESET

Jesus answered them, "It is not the healthy who need a doctor,
but the sick. I have not come to call the righteous,
but sinners to repentance."
Luke 5:31-32 (NIV)

Wouldn't it be nice if life came with a reset button, kind of like a video game? Where you are moving along just doing what you do, except when you get to a point where things aren't going the way you like, you can simply hit "reset" to wipe the slate clean, move in another direction, and then work toward the outcome you want. Well, through the processes of forgiveness, repentance, and reconciliation, a reset is a viable option. I am confident that most of us will fall into one or two categories when it comes to the topics of forgiveness, repentance, and reconciliation. The first category is those who have heard each of these words before, but have dismissed them as quickly as they were mentioned. The second category is for those who, through some church experiences, are at least familiar with each of these words. Well, it is time for us to move beyond simply hearing these words or being familiar with them to taking a deep dive to uncover what they are really about. Let's begin with forgiveness.

Forgiveness is a release of the feelings of resentment toward someone who has done you wrong. Just to make sure we are clear, the "someone" can also be yourself. I have discovered over the years that at times it has actually been easier for me to forgive others as opposed to forgiving myself. Nonetheless, it is imperative that we master the ability to forgive ourselves as well as others. Forgiveness is such an important subject that the word "forgive" appears 121 times in the Bible. If that is not enough to convince you, here are a few additional facts that stress the importance of forgiveness. First of all, God said to forgive. That's right, Matthew 6:14-15 says, "For if you forgive other people when they sin against you, your heavenly Father will also forgive you. But if you do not forgive others their sins, your Father will not forgive your sins" (NIV). The next reason is because as brothers and sisters in Christ, we are to love one another as Christ Jesus loves us. It is darn near impossible to love someone you have beef with. Lastly, like a reset button on our video games, forgiveness wipes the slate clean for everyone involved, which then opens the door to repentance.

Now, repentance takes that clean slate and runs with it in a different direction—God's direction. See, it is one thing to release those feelings of resentment, but now we have to be committed to doing things differently by moving away from those things or people that steered us off course in the first place. Repentance has the power to not only make us feel better, but to also change us from the inside out. It helps us commit, and stay committed, to turning away from doing things by the world's standard, and turn back to doing things by God's standard, in spite of anything we may have done in the past. I know what you're thinking, "Like really, *anything*? But you don't know what I've done or what I have been through." Then check out Acts 3:19 where the power of repentance is on full display. Peter is talking to the very people who killed Jesus. That's right—Jesus! He says, "Now repent of your sins and turn to God, so that your sins may be wiped away. Then times of refreshment will come from the presence of the Lord, and He will again send you Jesus, your appointed Messiah" (NLT). So, while you are correct that I do not know your past, I do know that Jesus has appealed to the Father, on behalf of all of us, not to hold our sins against us if we will repent and follow Him. This makes reconciliation possible.

Reconciliation reunites us with Christ and brings us into relationship. It tells sin to hit the road, and to take his cousins—guilt and shame—with him, and to lose our contact information. As a result, we become free from our past sins, and aware of and receptive to allowing God to order our steps and direction, which ultimately allows us to live in harmony with one another.

So, imagine a world without gossip, backbiting, or shade being thrown, replaced with people that lift each other up and encourage each other to be who God has created them to be. Well, let's stop dreaming and start doing exactly that. Let's be determined to not let another second pass by without forgiving ourselves, as well as others, for past offenses. Let's intentionally turn away from the world and back to being led solely by God, going deeper in relationship with our heavenly Father. When this happens, pressing "reset" not only gives us the hope needed to begin again, but also the ability to disciple other people to do the same.

LET'S TALK ABOUT IT

1. **Forgiveness:** What are some past experiences you are holding onto that are keeping you from being free to be who God has called you to be? What steps do you need to take in order to let these things go?

2. **Repentance:** We are all guilty of wanting to go in our own direction, or the direction that the world tells us we need to

go. However, what steps must we take in order to move in the right direction, God's direction, with Him doing the leading and us doing the following?

3. **Reconciliation:** What relationships (personally or professionally) can be reconciled as a result of us being in relationship with our Lord and Savior, Jesus Christ?

GO TELL THAT

Luke 23:34 (NIV)

Jesus said, "Father, forgive them, for they do not know what they are doing." And they divided up his clothes by casting lots.

Ephesians 4:32 (NIV)

Be kind and compassionate to one another, forgiving each other, just as in Christ God forgave you.

Hebrews 12:14 (NIV)

Make every effort to live in peace with everyone and to be holy; without holiness no one will see the Lord.

Romans 5:10 (NIV)

For if, while we were God's enemies, we were reconciled to him through the death of his Son, how much more, having been reconciled, shall we be saved through his life!

DAY 17
RANDOM ACTS OF KINDNESS

But when you do a charitable deed,
do not let your left hand know what your right hand is doing.
Matthew 6:3 (NKJV)

In our current culture, where so many people feel compelled through one form of social media or another to share everything they are doing, every second of the day as they do it, I encourage you to be aware of daily opportunities to perform random acts of kindness. Random acts of kindness take place when we are being intentional to show the love of Christ by doing something kind for another person within the flow of everyday life, and without posting it on social media. In other words, it is between God, us, and the recipient of love. In fact, the intent is what makes it so special. Unlike social media "likes" or attention that is bestowed upon us by other individuals, random acts of kindness are works that positively point others to the cross and its power, while keeping the attention and glory where it belongs—on God.

After all, it's human nature to feel a connection that creates a special bond when someone does something really meaningful for you. While that's not meant to be harmful, if we are not careful, it can lead to idol worship in the form of us wanting to be like someone else, or vice versa. However, as Christians, we know that the only person we are supposed to strive to be more like is Christ. So that means in order to even *lead* someone properly, we must be an even better *follower* of Christ. In 1 Corinthians 11:1, Paul says, "And you should

25

imitate me, just as I imitate Christ" (NLT). Let's be intentional to exemplify random acts of kindness as much as possible, for as many people as possible, so that the love of Christ can be felt by those we come in contact with on a daily basis. And as a result of our use of discretion, the credit will have to go to where it rightfully belongs, our heavenly Father, who alone is worthy of all the praise.

LET'S TALK ABOUT IT

1. Our motives play a huge role in regard to why we do the things we do. Think about some of the things you do often, and ask yourself if your motives are in alignment with the word of God.

2. We live in a world where technology allows us to be connected, literally, 24 hours a day. However, in regard to relationships, there has never been a time in history when we are more disconnected as people. What can you do today for someone else that can be used as a bridge to share with them your relationship with Christ?

3. What guidelines or reminders can you put in place to ensure that random acts of kindness are not an isolated event, but something you strive to do daily?

GO TELL THAT

1 Corinthians 3:7 (NIV)

So neither the one who plants nor the one who waters is anything, but only God, who makes things grow.

John 3:30 (NIV)

He must become greater; I must become less.

1 Corinthians 10:31 (NIV)

So whether you eat or drink or whatever you do, do it all for the glory of God.

DAY 16
LET'S TALK ABOUT SEX

1 Corinthians 6:12-20 <u>Flee Sexual Immorality (ESV)</u>
1 Corinthians 7:1-16 <u>Principles of Marriage</u> (ESV)

In the year 1990, the group Salt-N-Pepa came out with the hit song, "Let's Talk About Sex." The chorus went like this:

"Let's talk about sex baby,
Let's talk about you and me."[6]

So, with that in mind, let's do exactly that. Let's talk about sex. But in regard to what the Bible says about it. Contrary to what the current culture of "Netflix and chill" or "sliding into the DMs" may suggest, you were created for more than abusing your body for hookups and one night stands. Notice, I did not say *using* your body, but instead, *abusing* your body, because there is a difference. Abuse is the improper use of someone or something. It means to be used outside of the original purpose for which something was created. It is bad and inappropriate. On the other hand, to *use* someone or something is to take, hold, or deploy as a means of accomplishing a purpose or achieving a result. In essence, the difference between "abuse" and "use" lies in the intent. So, since God created us, in order to find out the original purpose He has for us in regard to sex, we must examine what He has to say about it within His word, the Holy Bible.

1 Corinthians 6:19-20 says,

---

6   Salt-N-Pepa 1990

"Don't you realize that your body is the temple of the Holy Spirit, who lives in you and was given to you by God? You do not belong to yourself, for God bought you with a high price. So you must honor God with your body" (NLT).

This means our bodies have been created by Christ on purpose, and *for* His purpose, to be a temple. The temple in biblical times was a visual representation to the people of a physical place where the presence and power of God dwelled. It was a place to be honored and treated with respect and of great value. Likewise, our bodies are to be honored and respected to the point that the Holy Spirit can reside within us in order to transform us. In addition to actual ownership, our bodies are in alignment with the principle of stewardship because they belong to God, but are to be taken care of by us. Wait, you mean my body is not mine to be used as I see fit? Nope, it belongs to God. In fact, in addition to Him creating us, He also purchased each of us back from the bondage of sin for a *high price*! What was the high price, you ask? The blood of Christ, which means the debt of sin that all of humanity once owed—me, you, and everyone—has been paid in full by the blood of Christ! Think about it this way: If God, our Creator and heavenly Father, can do all that for us, obedience to Him is the least we can do, right? As a result, we are to follow His instructions to honor Him with our bodies, which are the temples in which the Holy Spirit is to reside. Now I know you're thinking, "Is it really that deep?" or "Does it take all of that?" or "Does this Bible stuff even apply to the current sexual temptations and lust we deal with?" The answer to all of these questions is a resounding, "Yes!"

As God blesses each of us to gain wisdom as we get older, we get to personally experience what Ecclesiastes 1:9 says,

"History merely repeats itself. It has all been done before. Nothing under the sun is truly new" (NLT).

Likewise, dealing with lust and sexual desires is nothing new. So God, being the loving Father that He is, has provided[7] us an answer that addresses this issue once and for all in 1 Corinthians 6:12-20, which deals with how to flee sexual immorality, and in 1 Corinthians 7:1-16, which outlines the principles of marriage. At the end of this lesson, I have included both scriptures so you can read them. But right now, I'll provide you with the Cliffs Notes version. In biblical times, the people were also dealing with the same lustful desires that you and I still struggle with today. So, because God didn't want lust to consume them and turn their hearts from serving Him, God created and defined the institution of marriage as a means for both men and women to be able to fulfill their physical need for sex. Here's the kicker though. He, being a God of order, clearly defines marriage as being one man and one woman surrendering themselves before Christ in commitment to becoming one. Now, this is a really good place to pause for a quick PSA[8].

> Therefore, any union that is not in alignment with God's standard, even if it's lawful by the world's standard, isn't marriage as defined by God. Point blank and simple. Now let's get back to this sex and commitment thing.

As a result of the commitment of marriage, sex changed from being a bad thing to being a beautiful thing. Yep, you heard it here first. Sex, and lots of sex, is more than okay with God. In fact, as long as it occurs within the institution of marriage, it's beautiful. Sex is the means through which a husband and wife physically express their

---

7 Jehovah Jireh (pronounced Yireh) = the Lord will provide

8 Public Service Announcement

love for one another. And I know you remember Genesis 1:28, that whole thing about being fruitful and multiplying. Well, sex by married couples is how we were designed to produce fruit and multiply. So, marriage is the solution God gave us back then and it is still applicable right now. My prayer for you is that you will trust God to bring you that Mr. or Mrs. Right that He has made just for you, and instead of putting on a condom or engaging in other uses of birth control, you will commit to putting on a wedding ring. Then you can have at it all you want in regard to sex with your husband or wife. This may sound corny to some, but the truth of the matter is, as Christians, we should live in obedience to God's word. I'll conclude by asking a question of prioritization: "Which is more important? What God knows about you or what people think about you?" Your actions moving forward, especially in the area of sexual promiscuity or abstinence, will speak louder than anything you can ever say. I love you and am praying for you, but your heavenly Father loves you much more and wants the best for you. Sex with your spouse is the best it can get!

LET'S TALK ABOUT IT

1. What makes abstaining from sex until marriage so difficult?
2. Why is it that striving to live a life of purity until marriage is viewed as being corny or not cool?
3. In 1 Corinthians 6:19-20, the Bible clearly tells us that our bodies are not even our own. They belong to the Lord. But, if you are like me and stumbled by having sex before marriage, what are some steps you can take to get back on track—to stop abusing your body, and to start using your body to honor God by living a life of sexual purity?

GO TELL THAT

1 Corinthians 6:12-20 (ESV)

"All things are lawful for me," but not all things are helpful. "All things are lawful for me," but I will not be dominated by anything. "Food is meant for the stomach and the stomach for food"—and God will destroy both one and the other. The body is not meant for sexual immorality, but for the Lord, and the Lord for the body. And God raised the Lord and will also raise us up by his power. Do you not know that your bodies are members of Christ? Shall I then take the members of Christ and make them members of a prostitute? Never! Or do you not know that he who is joined to a prostitute becomes one body with her? For, as it is written, "The two will become one flesh." But he who is joined to the Lord becomes one spirit with him. Flee from sexual immorality. Every other sin a person commits is outside the body, but the sexually immoral person sins against his own body. Or do you not know that your body is a temple of the Holy Spirit within you, whom you have from God? You are not your own, for you were bought with a price. So glorify God in your body.

1 Corinthians 7:1-16 (ESV)

Now concerning the matters about which you wrote: "It is good for a man not to have sexual relations with a woman." But because of the temptation to sexual immorality, each man should have his own wife and each woman her own husband. The husband should give to his wife her conjugal rights, and likewise the wife to her husband. For the wife does not have authority over her own body, but the husband does. Likewise the husband does not have authority over his own body, but the wife does. Do not deprive one another, except perhaps by agreement for a limited time, that you may devote yourselves to prayer; but then come together again, so that Satan may not tempt you because of your lack of self-control.

Now as a concession, not a command, I say this. I wish that all were as I myself am. But each has his own gift from God, one of one kind and one of another.

To the unmarried and the widows I say that it is good for them to remain single, as I am. But if they cannot exercise self-control, they should marry. For it is better to marry than to burn with passion.

To the married I give this charge (not I, but the Lord): the wife should not separate from her husband (but if she does, she should remain unmarried or else be reconciled to her husband), and the husband should not divorce his wife.

To the rest I say (I, not the Lord) that if any brother has a wife who is an unbeliever, and she consents to live with him, he should not divorce her. If any woman has a husband who is an unbeliever, and he consents to live with her, she should not divorce him. For the unbelieving husband is made holy because of his wife, and the unbelieving wife is made holy because of her husband. Otherwise your children would be unclean, but as it is, they are holy. But if the unbelieving partner separates, let it be so. In such cases the brother or sister is not enslaved. God has called you to peace. For how do you know, wife, whether you will save your husband? Or how do you know, husband, whether you will save your wife?

Genesis 2:24 (NLT)

This explains why a man leaves his father and mother and is joined to his wife, and the two are united into one.

Proverbs 5:17-20 (MSG)

Your spring water is for you and you only,
   not to be passed around among strangers.
Bless your fresh-flowing fountain!
   Enjoy the wife you married as a young man!
Lovely as an angel, beautiful as a rose—
   don't ever quit taking delight in her body.
   Never take her love for granted!
Why would you trade enduring intimacies for cheap thrills with a
   whore?
   for dalliance with a promiscuous stranger?

DAY 15
INTOXICATED

Don't be drunk with wine, because that will ruin your life.
Instead, be filled with the Holy Spirit.
Ephesians 5:18 (NLT)

In the United States, there is this unwritten law that when you turn 21 years old, the ability to drink legally makes you an "official adult." In fact, many youngsters waste their 21st birthdays partying and drinking to commemorate this pitiful milestone of achievement. Until then, countless others—"minors" as the law categorizes them, those under the age of 21—waste time and risk their lives trying to indulge their desires to eat from the proverbial "forbidden fruit,"[9] the poisonous tree of alcohol. As a result, people (that would be us: me, you, or anyone who has decided to take a drink of alcohol) are consciously making choices to exchange their freedom for bondage and addiction. Wait, hold on, it's not even that deep, right? Bondage, addiction? That is not what anyone of us is thinking about when we take a drink, is it? No, we are just drinking to relax, for social purposes, or to manage the stress, right? Isn't that what we think we are doing? But here's a question I have for you. If what you are believing is not true, would you want to know? Well, since God has blessed me with a big mouth, I am going to tell you anyway.

Let's begin with the Bible, which, after all, is the absolute truth. Ephesians 5:18 says, "Don't be drunk with wine, because that will ruin your life. Instead, be filled with the Holy Spirit" (NLT). Raise your

---

9   A thing that is desired all the more because it is not allowed.

hand as high as possible if, when you take a drink of alcohol, your plan is to ruin your life. Now, unlike God, I am not omnipotent[10], omniscient[11], or omnipresent[12], but I am pretty darn sure you did not raise your hand. If that's the case, then why would you risk ruining your life over a temporary buzz? It doesn't make sense, but yet, this is what happens all the time, and here is why. See, we have been misled and lied to in regard to the goals of being an adult. Independence is what the world tells us makes us an adult, but the Bible tells us that *total dependence on God* is what we should strive for. The world celebrates pride and arrogance, but the Bible celebrates meekness and humility. As a result, we indulge in alcohol consumption, in spite of the risks, because our pride and arrogance embolden us to believe that although this happens to countless amounts of other people, that it can't happen to us. Well, we know what the Bible says about pride and arrogance, right? That "pride goes before destruction, and haughtiness before a fall"[13] (NLT). Therefore, let's make a declaration today to move forward in a different direction by taking this pledge.

I (fill in your name) pledge to
no longer risk the very freedom that Christ died on the cross to
secure for me, by abstaining from the use of alcohol, or any other
mind-altering substance.
I will no longer silently or idly sit by and watch others
continue to make the same mistake.
I will, by the grace of God and through His strength, use
my voice to fight to be heard by my fellow brothers and sisters

---

10 Having unlimited power; able to do anything.
11 Knowing everything.
12 Present everywhere at the same time.
13 Proverbs 16:18 (NLT)

until they choose to join me in this declaration of independence
from the use of alcohol, or any other mind-altering substance.
As a result, God will get the glory and we will live our
lives as He has ordained us to do—so filled with the Holy Spirit
that there will not be room for anything else.

LET'S TALK ABOUT IT

1. There is a quote that says, "If you don't stand for something, then you will fall for anything." When it comes to your stance on alcohol consumption, what is it that makes you feel the way you do?

2. If you gave up the consumption of alcohol, what exactly do you think you would lose or miss out on? What, in fact, would you gain?

3. As children of God, there are many times when we are called to do things or make sacrifices for the benefit of others. So, in essence, that means that this may not even be about you, but for someone else. Who do you know that could benefit from you taking a stance to abstain from the use of alcohol or any other mind-altering substance?

GO TELL THAT

Proverbs 20:1 (NIV)

Wine is a mocker and beer a brawler;
  whoever is led astray by them is not wise.

Proverbs 23:31-32 (NIV)

Do not gaze at wine when it is red,
  when it sparkles in the cup,
  when it goes down smoothly!
In the end it bites like a snake
  and poisons like a viper.

1 Corinthians 5:11 (NIV)

But now I am writing to you that you must not associate with anyone who claims to be a brother or sister but is sexually immoral or greedy, an idolater or slanderer, a drunkard or swindler. Do not even eat with such people.

Romans 13:13 (NIV)

Let us behave decently, as in the daytime, not in carousing and drunkenness, not in sexual immorality and debauchery, not in dissension and jealousy.

DAY 14
IN DUE TIME

So let's not get tired of doing what is good. At just the right time we will reap a harvest of blessing if we don't give up.
Galatians 6:9 (NLT)

Doesn't it seem like when you look around the only ones that are getting ahead are the people who are living contrary to the word of God? Not only does it seem like those who live with no regard to the Bible are winning, their lives also seem so much easier. They do not seem to be confined by a laundry list of things they cannot do, cannot say, certain ways they are supposed to act, or places they cannot go. However, if we are not careful, we can fall prey to the lie that the world is aggressively selling, of doing what you want, when you want, and how you want, with no thought of eternal consequences. Now I don't know about you, but "eternal" sounds like a really long time to me. So, let's lean on scripture to discuss how the Lord says we should handle this situation that all of us who are striving to live a life that is pleasing to God will be in more times than we can count.

Galatians 6:9, says

"So let's not get tired of doing what is good. At just the right time we will reap a harvest of blessing if we don't give up" (NLT).

The word "tired" here implies growing weary or becoming worn down by all the negative peer pressure that can accompany standing up for Christ within our world. Like with our physical bodies, in order to prevent us from *spiritually* wearing down or fatiguing, there are certain things we must do. The first thing we need to do is get our proper rest. Physical sleep is how we rest our bodies, but as Christians we don't just rest in the flesh. We rest spiritually in the Lord. The "A" clause of Psalm 37:7 says, "Rest in the LORD, and wait patiently for Him" (KJV). Next, we need to eat a proper spiritual diet. This consists of us reading our Bibles daily so we can digest the word of God as the food for our souls that it is intended to be. Then, we must operate as if we know that all of the word of God will come to pass.

In addition, "at just the right time" speaks to the finality of God's timing. This means as His children we need to get comfortable, and stay comfortable, with the fact that God's timing is not our timing. God's timing is *always* better than our timing. Think about it this way: We show our earthly parents respect when they tell us we cannot have something right now. Then, how much more should we respect our heavenly Father's timing? After all, Numbers 23:19 does say, "God is not a man, so he does not lie" (NLT). However, while we wait, we do not wait idly. No, we do so by sowing seeds daily with the expectation that God will bring them to fruition in the form of us reaping future blessings. That means instead of needing to hear "good job" or "well done" from our peers, we find comfort in waiting for a better reward—God's reward. However, none of this will be possible if we throw in the towel. As the quote attributed to Winston Churchill says, and I will add the word "worldly" at the beginning for emphasis: [Worldly] "success is not final, failure is not fatal: it's the courage to continue that counts." Now, the choice is yours. But my prayer is that you will be encouraged in the Lord, be content with His timing, fight the good fight, and refuse to give up until our heavenly Father calls you home.

LET'S TALK ABOUT IT

1. Reflect upon a time when you asked God for something you felt you really needed, but He did not give you what you asked for, or did not give it to you when you asked for it. How did that make you feel?

2. What are some reasons why God does not give us what we want, when we want it?

3. What is your personal view of God, and how does the way we view God affect the way we live our daily lives? For instance, is He a genie that is at our beck and call to grant us our wishes, or is He the Sovereign Ruler of the world, which includes our lives?

GO TELL THAT

Psalm 37:7 (KJV)

Rest in the Lord, and wait patiently for him: fret not thyself because of him who prospereth in his way, because of the man who bringeth wicked devices to pass.

Numbers 23:19 (NLT)

God is not a man, so he does not lie.

He is not human, so he does not change his mind.

Has he ever spoken and failed to act?

Has he ever promised and not carried it through?

DAY 13
I CHOOSE LOVE

We love because he first loved us.
1 John 4:19 (NIV)

The internet, as well as social media, provides us the ability to stay connected to one another. This isn't a bad thing as some would suggest, but this also is not the greatest invention since sliced bread. Like all things that God has created[14], these are intended to be good, but it all depends on the intent of the person being good as well. For example, both the internet and social media can provide us with unlimited, around-the-clock information that gives us the opportunity to stay informed with what is going on in our local and global communities. In addition, social media provides an opportunity to maintain, establish, and grow both personal and professional relationships. However, when I stop to observe what is going on in our country and, better yet, our world, I see a great deal of hurting people who are then turning around and hurting other people. I see divisiveness being encouraged over unity. I see the unique differences that each of us has been given intentionally by our Creator—differences of race, sizes, and beliefs—fueling discord among fellow citizens. Probably most disturbing is the openness in which hate is being justified on television, on the internet, and over blogs and online message boards. Well, that stops today! As Jacqueline Kennedy said of her late husband, John F. Kennedy, "He believed that one man can make a difference–and that every man

---

14 Since everything God created is good, we should not reject any of it but receive it with thanks. (1 Timothy 4:4 NLT)

should try." So, I have decided that there is enough hate in the world. I choose love, and my prayer is that you will join me on this mission.

Our mission is to be intentional about showing the love of Christ by how we treat others. Our purpose is to create a legacy of individuals who intentionally choose to love one another as opposed to hate. Our teammates are those who are also fed up with the divisiveness, hate, and negativity that is affecting all aspects of our society. Our mission fields will be our homes, our churches, our communities, workplaces, and anywhere we come in contact with our fellow brothers and sisters in Christ. We will be intentional to imitate the greatest leader to ever live, Jesus Christ—To live on purpose, with the purpose of pleasing God. While this definitely won't be easy, it will be worth it. I *emphatically* choose love! Do you?

LET'S TALK ABOUT IT

1. What is your initial response to all the divisiveness that seems to be overwhelmingly accepted and encouraged in our present culture?

2. As Jacqueline Kennedy said of her late husband, John F. Kennedy, "He believed that one man can make a difference- and that every man should try." What is preventing you from being that "one" man or woman who becomes the catalyst for change?

3. What are some ways you can use your current, God-given social media platforms to connect with others to encourage them to choose love, as well as help others do the same?

GO TELL THAT

1 Corinthians 11:1 (NLT)

And you should imitate me, just as I imitate Christ.

Isaiah 58:9-12 (MSG)

"If you get rid of unfair practices,
  quit blaming victims,
  quit gossiping about other people's sins,
If you are generous with the hungry
  and start giving yourselves to the down-and-out,
Your lives will begin to glow in the darkness,
  your shadowed lives will be bathed in sunlight.
I will always show you where to go.
  I'll give you a full life in the emptiest of places—
  firm muscles, strong bones.
You'll be like a well-watered garden,
  a gurgling spring that never runs dry.
You'll use the old rubble of past lives to build anew,
  rebuild the foundations from out of your past.
You'll be known as those who can fix anything,
  restore old ruins, rebuild and renovate,
  make the community livable again."

Ephesians 2:10 (NIV)

For we are God's handiwork, created in Christ Jesus to do good works, which God prepared in advance for us to do.

THE MOVEMENT — WE CHOOSE LOVE

And you should imitate me, just as I imitate Christ.
1 Corinthians 11:1 (NLT)

To honor the memory of George Floyd, Breonna Taylor, Ahmaud Arbery, and countless others who've been victims of racial discrimination, bigotry, and social injustice, the Charleston Southern Football ministry has decided that there is enough hate in this world. So...

We Choose Love

We Choose Love is a movement that presents each of us with an opportunity to put action behind our emotions by confronting injustices head on. Our mission is to be intentional about showing the love of Christ by how we treat one another for the purpose of contributing to a legacy of individuals who intentionally choose to love others as opposed to hate. Our teammates are those who are also fed up with divisiveness, discrimination, bigotry, and injustices of any kind. We will do this by imitating the greatest leader to ever live, Jesus Christ, and choosing to love unconditionally as He does. Now, here is where the rubber meets the road because, like in sports, this becomes a condition of the heart. Are we willing to continue to define people by their skin color, socioeconomic class, and occupations? Or can we dig deeper than we have ever had to dig to see them as another human being created in the image of God, and use our differences as a way to expand our experiences? My prayer is that the latter can happen. By no means will this be easy or will this happen overnight. In fact, it is going to take each of us to make a daily choice to be the change we want to see. We have to continue to persevere even when we feel like the change to come is slow, but it will definitely be worth it. So, if you are wondering what's next or where we go from here as a country, then join us as **We Choose Love** by redefining our homes, our communities, and our country, one God-honoring interaction at a time. **#WeChooseLove**

DAY 12
EVERYDAY HEROES OF FAITH

Don't forget to show hospitality to strangers, for some who have done this have entertained angels without realizing it!
Hebrews 13:2 (NLT)

If we are not careful to guard our hearts and minds in regard to the constant negative messages and images that are out there, we will miss the opportunities to celebrate real-life heroes of faith. That's right. Heroes of faith are not just found in the pages of the Bible. Through the indwelling of the Holy Spirit, there are people around us that, on a daily basis, are faithfully functioning as the hands and feet of Christ. For me and anyone who has the privilege of walking into the Publix Supermarket at Winston Park in Coconut Creek, Florida, Ms. Pam stacks up with the best of the Bible heroes.

Ms. Pam is a beautiful child of God who works as a cashier, but clearly understands that her position is her platform on which she can spread the love of God to everyone she comes in contact with. Immediately when you approach the cashier area, you can hear the difference. From the time a customer walks into her line, the first thing you notice is a huge smile that is like the doorway to an even bigger heart. She greets each customer by letting them know how much she loves them and how appreciative she is for them choosing her line. Next, she explains to the customer that is next in line that she will be with them in a moment. Her humility and love for Christ are on full display all the time. In fact, my family and I no longer live in the area, but every time we visit, I am intentional about going to Publix just so I can have an encounter with this giant of faith in action.

When I look at Ms. Pam, I see the best of humanity. A person who is not afraid to lead with love, which literally brings tears to my eyes. This by no means implies that Ms. Pam is perfect or without her own set of unique flaws. However, it gives me hope to see that our God is so awesome that He can take flawed, imperfect individuals—such as Ms. Pam, me, and you, if we are willing—and can transform us into vessels through which hope and love can flow in abundance. The key is we must make ourselves available to be used by Him. Now to most people, this is where the intimidation and fear kick in because of the misconception that there is a litany of prerequisites that must be fulfilled before God can use you. So, let me set the record straight once and for all. God isn't looking for perfection. What He is looking for are individuals who love Him so much that they are also willing to love His people. Will you dare to make yourself available for God's purposes? Will you, like Ms. Pam, become a hero of faith by allowing the Holy Spirit to transform you to be the hands and feet of Christ, and by courageously sharing His love every day with everyone?

LET'S TALK ABOUT IT

1. Take a few moments and think about the names of some everyday heroes of faith that you have encountered.
2. What obstacles, fears, or apprehensions are preventing you from fully surrendering to God so He can use you for His will to be done?
3. Now that you have identified the obstacles that are preventing you from being used by God, what steps will you take to elim-

inate them? What is your timetable for getting started? My prayer is that you decide that your time is now!

GO TELL THAT

Hebrews 11:1-40 (NLT)

Faith shows the reality of what we hope for; it is the evidence of things we cannot see. Through their faith, the people in days of old earned a good reputation.

By faith we understand that the entire universe was formed at God's command, that what we now see did not come from anything that can be seen.

It was by faith that Abel brought a more acceptable offering to God than Cain did. Abel's offering gave evidence that he was a righteous man, and God showed his approval of his gifts. Although Abel is long dead, he still speaks to us by his example of faith.

It was by faith that Enoch was taken up to heaven without dying—"he disappeared, because God took him." For before he was taken up, he was known as a person who pleased God. And it is impossible to please God without faith. Anyone who wants to come to him must believe that God exists and that he rewards those who sincerely seek him.

It was by faith that Noah built a large boat to save his family from the flood. He obeyed God, who warned him about things that had never happened before. By his faith Noah condemned the rest of the world, and he received the righteousness that comes by faith.

It was by faith that Abraham obeyed when God called him to leave home and go to another land that God would give him as his inheritance. He went without knowing where he was going. And even when he reached the land God promised him, he lived there by faith—for he was like a foreigner, living in tents. And so did Isaac and Jacob, who inherited the same promise. Abraham was confidently looking forward to a city with eternal foundations, a city designed and built by God.

It was by faith that even Sarah was able to have a child, though she was barren and was too old. She believed that God would keep his promise. And so a whole nation came from this one man who was as good as dead—a nation with so many people that, like the stars in the sky and the sand on the seashore, there is no way to count them.

All these people died still believing what God had promised them. They did not receive what was promised, but they saw it all from a distance and welcomed it. They agreed that they were foreigners and nomads here on earth. Obviously people who say such things are looking forward to a country they can call their own. If they had longed for the country they came from, they could have gone back. But they were looking for a better place, a heavenly homeland. That is why God is not ashamed to be called their God, for he has prepared a city for them.

It was by faith that Abraham offered Isaac as a sacrifice when God was testing him. Abraham, who had received God's promises, was ready to sacrifice his only son, Isaac, even though God had told him, "Isaac is the son through whom your descendants will be counted." Abraham reasoned that if Isaac died, God was able to bring him back to life again. And in a sense, Abraham did receive his son back from the dead.

It was by faith that Isaac promised blessings for the future to his sons, Jacob and Esau.

It was by faith that Jacob, when he was old and dying, blessed each of Joseph's sons and bowed in worship as he leaned on his staff.

It was by faith that Joseph, when he was about to die, said confidently that the people of Israel would leave Egypt. He even commanded them to take his bones with them when they left.

It was by faith that Moses' parents hid him for three months when he was born. They saw that God had given them an unusual child, and they were not afraid to disobey the king's command.

It was by faith that Moses, when he grew up, refused to be called the son of Pharaoh's daughter. He chose to share the oppression of God's people instead of enjoying the fleeting pleasures of sin. He thought it was better to suffer for the sake of Christ than to own the treasures of Egypt, for he was looking ahead to his great reward. It was by faith that Moses left the land of Egypt, not fearing the king's anger. He kept right on going because he kept his eyes on the one who is invisible. It was by faith that Moses commanded the people of Israel to keep the Passover and to sprinkle blood on the doorposts so that the angel of death would not kill their firstborn sons.

It was by faith that the people of Israel went right through the Red Sea as though they were on dry ground. But when the Egyptians tried to follow, they were all drowned.

It was by faith that the people of Israel marched around Jericho for seven days, and the walls came crashing down.

It was by faith that Rahab the prostitute was not destroyed with the people in her city who refused to obey God. For she had given a friendly welcome to the spies.

How much more do I need to say? It would take too long to recount the stories of the faith of Gideon, Barak, Samson, Jephthah, David, Samuel, and all the prophets. By faith these people overthrew kingdoms, ruled with justice, and received what God had promised them. They shut the mouths of lions, quenched the flames of fire, and escaped death by the edge of the sword. Their weakness was turned to strength. They became strong in battle and put whole armies to flight. Women received their loved ones back again from death.

But others were tortured, refusing to turn from God in order to be set free. They placed their hope in a better life after the resurrection. Some were jeered at, and their backs were cut open with whips. Others were chained in prisons. Some died by stoning, some were sawed in half, and others were killed with the sword. Some went about wearing skins of sheep and goats, destitute and oppressed and mistreated. They were too good for this world, wandering over deserts and mountains, hiding in caves and holes in the ground.

All these people earned a good reputation because of their faith, yet none of them received all that God had promised. For God had something better in mind for us, so that they would not reach perfection without us.

DAY 11
HEADPHONES AND SMARTPHONES: THE CURRENT DOORWAYS TO SECRET SINS

Whatever you have said in the dark will be heard in the light, and what you have whispered behind closed doors will be shouted from the housetops for all to hear!
Luke 12:3 (NLT)

Secret sins are those things we struggle to control when we are all alone. Well, when you think about it, since God is omnipotent, omniscient, and omnipresent, we are never really alone. But again, secret sins are those things that we do in private when we feel no one else is watching. They are the things that if, by chance, someone else found out about them, would cause feelings of shame, embarrassment, or guilt. In fact, just the thought of these things coming to light causes all types of anxiety and fear. Now here is where the enemy comes in, who, by the way, is the biggest liar there is. No really, he literally is. John 8:44 says, "When he lies, he speaks his native language, for he is a liar and the father of lies" (NIV). This lowdown, conniving liar rolls up on us under the alias of concealment to get us to feel that secret sins are okay. Spewing foolishness like, "Everybody is doing it." or "A little of this or a little of that has never hurt anyone." or "What you do is no one else's business." What's even more alarming than these blatant lies are the weapons he is choosing to use: headphones and smartphones!

53

Since concealment is the foundation that all secret sins are built upon, these two weapons are by far the most convenient, simply because they are everywhere and are being used by everyone. In addition to the many positive, legitimate uses that headphones and smartphones have, they also provide unlimited, around-the-clock access to things, such as pornography, explicit music and videos, inappropriate movie viewing, and all the trappings that the internet has to offer, free of interruption or accountability. Now, I am by no means saying that headphones and smartphones are evil and should be collected and burned at the stake. What I am being insistent about is that we stay alert and aware of the nature of the enemy, which is to take the good things that God has created and given to us to use for His glory, and, if he can't outright destroy them, then he will distort them. Let's be determined to not only be mindful of this ourselves, but to make sure our fellow brothers and sisters in Christ are also aware.

LET'S TALK ABOUT IT

1. Since God created all things and all things created by God are good, what are some of the good things that are currently being used for bad?
2. In lieu of avoiding these things altogether, what are some practices that can be put into place to ensure that we, or the ones we love, do not fall into the trap of misusing God's good things or creations?
3. There is a saying that goes, "When you know better, then you do better." As a result of this devotion, since we now know better, when is the time that we start doing better in regard to dealing with secret sins?

GO TELL THAT

Galatians 6:7 (NLT)

Don't be misled—you cannot mock the justice of God. You will always harvest what you plant.

Matthew 6:22-23 (NLT)

"Your eye is like a lamp that provides light for your body. When your eye is healthy, your whole body is filled with light. But when your eye is unhealthy, your whole body is filled with darkness. And if the light you think you have is actually darkness, how deep that darkness is!"

1 Peter 5:8 (NLT)

Stay alert! Watch out for your great enemy, the devil. He prowls around like a roaring lion, looking for someone to devour.

DAY 10
GREATNESS: GHEA –
GOD HONORING EFFORT
AND ATTITUDE

*Work with enthusiasm, as though you were working
for the Lord rather than for people.*
Ephesians 6:7 (NLT)

There are so many definitions and interpretations of what greatness is. The Merriam-Webster Dictionary[15] defines "greatness" as being "eminent, distinguished, markedly superior in character or quality, remarkably skilled." I love the definition and interpretation that gospel hip-hop artist and co-owner of the record label Reflective Music Group, Derek Minor, gives in regard to what biblical greatness is in his 2016 song titled, "Greatness." In the song, Derek states that since we are God's children who have been made in His image, when we reflect God, we reflect the image of greatness. Furthermore, we can be rest assured that God has purposed all of us for greatness in spite of what the world or our circumstances may try to imply.

As a result of being given this designation of greatness, that means that we are held to a higher standard: God's standard! That standard is the foundation for our definition of greatness outlined in the acronym GHEA, which means God Honoring Effort and Attitude. So, our definition of greatness is to give a God-honoring effort while having a God-honoring attitude in everything we do all the time. That means that as long as we have breath in our bodies, as long as God

---

15 Merriam-Webster Dictionary 2021 (online)

sees fit to wake us up in the morning, then it is unacceptable that we give anything less than our best in all that we do. All while also having a great attitude in the process. By God's standard, we are supposed to work hard and enjoy our work. Proverbs 17:22 says, "A cheerful disposition is good for your health; gloom and doom leave you bone-tired" (MSG). So, not only is a good attitude God-honoring, it literally helps you stay healthy. Therefore, whatever you do, wherever God has you, instead of being results driven, let's be process driven by being committed to biblical greatness, by giving a God-honoring effort while having a God-honoring attitude in everything we do all the time. If we can develop the habit of doing this consistently, by God's grace, the results will take care of themselves.

LET'S TALK ABOUT IT

1. Now that we have a definition of greatness that calls us to operate with a God-honoring effort while having a God-honoring attitude, what are some ways that we can model greatness within our daily lives?

2. How does knowing that God's standard is the standard to which we should strive to attain change the way we prepare?

3. What is the difference between being process driven as opposed to being results driven? What are some of the benefits?

GO TELL THAT

Ephesians 6:7-8 (NIV)

Serve wholeheartedly, as if you were serving the Lord, not people, because you know that the Lord will reward each one for whatever good they do, whether they are slave or free.

Colossians 3:23 (NIV)

Whatever you do, work at it with all your heart, as working for the Lord, not for human masters.

Ecclesiastes 5:18-20 (NIV)

This is what I have observed to be good: that it is appropriate for a person to eat, to drink and to find satisfaction in their toilsome labor under the sun during the few days of life God has given them—for this is their lot. Moreover, when God gives someone wealth and possessions, and the ability to enjoy them, to accept their lot and be happy in their toil—this is a gift of God. They seldom reflect on the days of their life, because God keeps them occupied with gladness of heart.

DAY 9
FOR THE LOVE OF MONEY

For the love of money is the root of all kinds of evil.
And some people, craving money, have wandered from the true
faith and pierced themselves with many sorrows.
1 Timothy 6:10 (NLT)

The King James Version of the Holy Bible mentions money 140 times. In fact, the Bible devotes a good amount of attention to financial matters related to money or its equivalent, to the point where it is one of the most talked about subjects. Now, the common misconception is that when it comes to the Bible, money is a bad thing. This could not be further from the truth. In fact, within the messages of the Bible we see that God blessed Abraham[16], Isaac[17], Job[18], Solomon[19], Joseph[20], and David[21] by showing all of them the money or its equivalent. So, it is evident that money in and of itself is not bad. The *love* of money is where all the evil problems stem from.

The Merriam-Webster Dictionary[22] defines the word "love" as "an object of attachment, devotion, or admiration." So, the love of money means we become attached to the physical state of money.

---

16 Abraham was very rich in livestock, silver, and gold. (Genesis 13:2 NLT)

17 When Isaac planted his crops that year, he harvested a hundred times more grain than he planted, for the Lord blessed him. (Genesis 26:12 NLT)

18 When Job prayed for his friends, the Lord restored his fortunes. In fact, the Lord gave him twice as much as before! (Job 42:10 NLT)

19 So King Solomon became richer and wiser than any other king on earth. (1 Kings 10:23 NLT)

20 By selling grain to the people, Joseph eventually collected all the money in Egypt and Canaan, and he put the money in Pharaoh's treasury. (Genesis 47:14 NLT)

21 He died at a ripe old age, having enjoyed long life, wealth, and honor. Then his son Solomon ruled in his place. (1 Chronicles 29:28 NLT)

22 Merriam-Webster Dictionary 2021 (online)

In other words, we like having it on us in the form of cash or having access to it through our bank accounts. This causes us to devote the majority of our time and actions to accumulating more of it because we become focused on what it can do for us from a material standpoint, as well as the status it validates from the world's perspective. As a result of this skewed outlook, we begin to actively engage in idolatry by replacing our admiration for God with our admiration for money. So instead of operating within the divine order of operations as the Bible lays out—where we worship God, love people, and use things— the love of money turns this upside down and inside out to the point where we use people, love self, and worship stuff.

However, all hope is not lost. Each day, we have many opportunities to choose how we engage with money and to determine the role it plays in our lives. The first is to use money to honor God. We are to be good stewards of the financial blessings He so graciously gives us by faithfully paying our tithes. The second is to provide for the necessities of life that we need in order to live. Lastly, money is to be used as seeds to be sown into the lives of others so that we can be a blessing to as many people as possible. In the words of poet Henry David Thoreau, "The cost of a thing is the amount of what I will call life which is required to be exchanged for it." Let's stop short-changing ourselves by exchanging our time in the pursuit of the almighty dollar for an all-out pursuit of the Almighty God.

LET'S TALK ABOUT IT

1. Before reading this lesson, what was your view of money and how have you been prioritizing it within your life?
2. Since reading this lesson, has your view of money changed or remained the same?
3. What, if any, changes do you need to make to ensure that money remains in the proper place in your life and is being used for kingdom building?

GO TELL THAT

Matthew 19:23 (NIV)

Then Jesus said to his disciples, "Truly I tell you, it is hard for someone who is rich to enter the kingdom of heaven."

Matthew 6:24 (NIV)

"No one can serve two masters. Either you will hate the one and love the other, or you will be devoted to the one and despise the other. You cannot serve both God and money."

DAY 8
DISTRACTIONS

Watch and pray so that you will not fall into temptation.
Mark 14:38 (NLT)

There are very few guarantees in life, but here is one of them: As soon as you make your mind up to give your life to Christ, you can expect distractions to show up in full force. There are so many things that already compete for our attention, but because we often confuse activity with *productivity*, many of the things we waste time doing on a daily basis are merely distractions. Distractions, by design, have the sole purpose of getting us off course by clouding our vision to prevent us from reaching our goals. For instance, if we want to go from point A to point B, the only way to get off course is to take our eyes off of what we are pursuing. Now I know this sounds as if I am stating the obvious, but what makes distractions so difficult to avoid are their chameleon-like ability to disguise themselves as things that are appealing to us, such as promotions, procrastination, fear, sex, fake friends—especially on social media—and liberality in the form of freedoms of choice we all enjoy. In addition, distractions often prevent us from acknowledging and fully accepting our responsibilities.

So, let's discuss some of the responsibilities that we have. Of course, our standard is going to be God's standard. First, everyone has a responsibility to either abstain from sex before marriage or enjoy the pleasures of sex within the institution of marriage, as clearly defined by God. This can prove to be very difficult, but it is doable. In fact, the reason this is so difficult for most of us is because we have already fallen short in this area, which makes it that much harder to keep from falling again. Well, instead of dwelling on the past, let's examine some ways to move forward in order to do better. We must all be mindful to guard both our eyes and ears in regard to the things we are exposing ourselves to. Two areas that come to mind immediately are music and movies. Due to the huge amounts of time we spend watching movies and listening to music, we must make sure the things we are seeing and hearing are not creating improper images of the opposite sex. We have to practice both restraint and good judgment in regard to how these things influence our thoughts. Since thoughts precede actions, this will be key to us remaining sexually pure.

Next, we have a responsibility to avoid procrastination. This is one that is very prevalent among young people because it creates the false perception that you have time on your side, and that you can do things later that are meant to be done now. In other words, it douses any flicker of a flame that could light a fire under us in regard to our sense of urgency. So instead of being people of conviction and commitment, we become passive to the point of indecisiveness, to where being on the fence becomes our safe haven for everything. In the Bible, this is known as being "lukewarm," which means not being for something or against it, just on the fence. Well, here is how our Savior feels about lukewarm people. Revelation 3:15-16 says, "I know you inside and out, and find little to my liking. You're not cold, you're not hot–far better to be either cold or hot! You're stale. You're stagnant. You make me want to vomit" (MSG). Ouch! God isn't holding anything back. With just the thought of us knowing that our procrastination makes God sick to His stomach, we should all be ready for a little carpe diem, which, by the way, means "to seize the day."

With that being said, the order of the day moves to our responsibility of being good stewards of the financial blessings God has given us.. This includes both money and material possessions. I know you think you know why this is important, but I am going to share some additional thoughts on the matter with you anyway. If our perspective in regard to financial blessings is not right, we will operate as hoarders as opposed to overseers. This means our goals will move from being diligent and content with what God has given us to being consumed with accumulating more. Now in and of itself, money and possessions are not bad. As overseers, they are gifts from God. However, as hoarders, the love of money becomes the root of all evil, and that is not God's standard. That's the world's standard. This world is working overtime to convince us that our purpose in life is to get money so we can experience the best things in life that money can buy. Well, that could not be further from the truth. The truth is that hell and Heaven are both very real! The truth is that while we are saved by grace and not by our good works, as God's children, we have been saved *for* good works, which include being obedient overseers of the financial blessings God has so graciously given us. So, unlike the YOLO (you only live once) attitude, we look forward to living life beyond here on earth with God in eternity where we hope to hear, "Well done, good and faithful servant" (Matthew 25:23 KJV). As a result, my prayer is that, together, you and I will no longer allow ourselves or others to be victims of distractions by firmly keeping our eyes, hearts, and minds focused on the Lord, from whom all of our strength comes from.

LET'S TALK ABOUT IT

1. What are some of the distractions you encounter that you are allowing to take your eyes off your goal(s)?

2. Most goals fall into one of two categories: "me" goals, which are all about the things that benefit us, or "we" goals, things that benefit others as well as us. Take an inventory of your goals and determine which category your goal(s) fall into.

3. Now that you have identified distractions and categorized your goal(s), are they in alignment with what God's goals are for your life?

GO TELL THAT

Ephesians 5:31 (MSG)

And this is why a man leaves father and mother and cherishes his wife. No longer two, they become "one flesh."

1 Corinthians 7:8-9 (ESV)

To the unmarried and the widows I say that it is good for them to remain single, as I am. But if they cannot exercise self-control, they should marry. For it is better to marry than to burn with passion.

1 Thessalonians 4:3-5 (ESV)

For this is the will of God, your sanctification: that you abstain from sexual immorality; that each one of you know how to control his own body in holiness and honor, not in the passion of lust like the Gentiles who do not know God.

John 3:16 (NIV)

For God so loved the world that he gave his one and only Son, that whoever believes in him shall not perish but have eternal life.

Ephesians 2:8 (NLT)

God saved you by his grace when you believed. And you can't take credit for this; it is a gift from God.

DAY 7
DEBT

The rich rule over the poor, and the borrower is slave to the lender.
Proverbs 22:7 (NIV)

Back in the day, the rule of finance was very simple. If you couldn't afford to pay for something outright, that meant you could not afford it, and probably didn't need it. If by chance the desire to own whatever it was did not go away, then a person would develop a financial plan to acquire it. That plan would be based upon discipline and patience so that over time the item could be purchased without incurring debt. Well, with the abundance of credit available, that fundamental mind-set has changed to an overall thought process of, "If you can't afford it but want it, then simply charge it." If truth be told, that not only sounds like a recipe for disaster, it also works contrary to the word of God.

"The rich rule over the poor, and the borrower is slave to the lender" (Proverbs 22:7 NIV). As children of God, we are designed to enjoy a rich life[23] where we are not in bondage to anything or anyone[24]. Now, the word "rich" from a biblical standpoint is not measured by how much money we can accumulate, but by how faithful we are in regard to stewardship of the gifts God has blessed us with. So often there is confusion around what stewardship is, so for clarity on biblical stewardship, we are going to examine both the definition and the four principles of stewardship as outlined by the Institute for Faith,

---

23 "My purpose is to give them a rich and satisfying life." (John 10:10 NLT)
24 It is for freedom that Christ has set us free. Stand firm, then, and do not let yourselves be burdened again by a yoke of slavery. (Galatians 5:1 NIV)

Work & Economics. First, stewardship is defined as being where the concepts of faith, work, and economics intersect. Next, is the categorization of the principles as (1) ownership, (2) responsibility, (3) accountability, and (4) reward. Let's spend some time diving deeper into the application of each of these principles. The principle of *ownership* is first.

    1. The Principle of Ownership

        The psalmist begins the 24th psalm with,

        The earth is the LORD's, and everything in it, the world, and all who live in it.

        In the beginning of Genesis, God creates everything and puts Adam in the Garden to work it and to take care of it. It is clear that man was created to work, and that *work is the stewardship of all of the creation that God has given him.*

        This is the fundamental principle of biblical stewardship. God owns everything, we are simply managers or administrators acting on his behalf.

        Therefore, stewardship expresses our obedience regarding the administration of everything God has placed under our control, which is all encompassing. Stewardship is the commitment of one's self and possessions to God's service, recognizing that we do not have the right of control over our property or ourselves.

        Next, is the principle of *responsibility.*

    2. The Principle of Responsibility

        Although God gives us "all things richly to enjoy," nothing is ours. Nothing really belongs to us. God owns everything; we're responsible for how we treat it and what we do with it. While we complain about our rights here on earth, the Bible constantly asks, What about your responsibilities? Owners have rights; stewards have responsibilities.

We are called as God's stewards to manage that which belongs to God. While God has graciously entrusted us with the care, development, and enjoyment of everything he owns as his stewards, we are responsible to manage his holdings well and according to his desires and purposes.

Let's move on to the principle of *accountability.*

3. The Principle of Accountability

A steward is one who manages the possessions of another. We are all stewards of the resources, abilities and opportunities that God has entrusted to our care, and one day each one of us will be called to give an account for how we have managed what the Master has given us.

This is the maxim taught by the Parable of the Talents. God has entrusted authority over the creation to us and we are not allowed to rule over it as we see fit. We are called to exercise our dominion under the watchful eye of the Creator managing his creation in accord with the principles he has established.

Like the servants in the Parable of the Talents, we will be called to give an account of how we have administered everything we have been given, including our time, money, abilities, information, wisdom, relationships, and authority.

We will all give account to the rightful owner as to how well we managed the things he has entrusted to us.

Lastly, is the principle of reward.

4. The Principle of Reward

In Colossians 3:23-24 Paul writes:

Whatever you do, work at it with all your heart, as working for the Lord, not for men, since you know that you will receive an inheritance from the Lord as a reward. It is the Lord Christ you are serving.

The Bible shows us in the parables of the Kingdom that faithful stewards who do the master's will with the master's resources can expect to be rewarded incompletely in this life, but fully in the next.

We all should long to hear the master say what he exclaims in Matthew 25:21:

Well done, good and faithful servant! You have been faithful with a few things; I will put you in charge of many things. Come and share your master's happiness![25]

Therefore, faithful stewardship is the bridge that connects our ability to live rich lives with the freedom Jesus has given us through the shedding of His blood, without being in jeopardy of forfeiture, which comes from the strain that mismanagement of debt can cause.

LET'S TALK ABOUT IT

1. Who or what has influenced your views on how you see debt?
2. Are your views on debt in alignment with the word of God?
3. There is a saying that goes, "When you know better, then you do better." Now that you know what the word of God says in regard to debt, how can you now strive to be better in regard to (a) stewardship, (b) responsibility, (c) accountability, and (d) the expectation of reward?

---

25 Whelchel 2012

GO TELL THAT

Psalm 24:1-2 (NIV)

The earth is the LORD's, and everything in it,
  the world, and all who live in it;
for he founded it on the seas
  and established it on the waters.

Matthew 25:21 (NIV)

"Well done, good and faithful servant! You have been faithful with a few things; I will put you in charge of many things. Come and share your master's happiness!"

Colossians 3:23-24 (NIV)

Whatever you do, work at it with all your heart, as working for the Lord, not for human masters, since you know that you will receive an inheritance from the Lord as a reward. It is the Lord Christ you are serving.

John 10:10 (NLT)

My pupose is to give them a rich and satisfying life.

Galatians 5:1 (NIV)

It is for freedom that Christ has set us free. Stand firm, then, and do not let yourselves be burdened again by a yoke of slavery.

DAY 6
DEALING WITH ANXIETY

I bless GOD every chance I get;
my lungs expand with his praise.
I live and breathe GOD;
if things aren't going well, hear this and be happy:
Join me in spreading the news;
together let's get the word out.
Psalm 34:1-3 (MSG)

One of the many things I love about the word of God[26] is that it is designed to be our own personal GPS in regard to providing turn-by-turn directions and instructions about how to deal with the anxieties that will arise as we navigate through life. However, unlike doctors (who are very useful, I might add), we don't have to schedule an appointment or work around their office hours, which means we may or may not get treated for our conditions. In lieu of medication, we do not need a prescription and definitely do not have to deal with the side effects that come from any and all over-the-counter drugs. There is also no shame associated with acknowledging that, at times, even the strongest of us get worn down and need help. Nope, the word of God is both available and accessible to all who desire to know the truth and then live according to it. What's even more encouraging is that there are characters, living breathing people just like you and me, that went through the exact things back then that we are going through today. For instance, David, a man after God's own heart, dealt

---

26 The Holy Bible

with the anxiety of being unjustly pursued by King Saul, which led to him having to be on the run to avoid death. So, really fast, in case you missed it, that means that David, whom God anointed to be king, dealt with the following issues:

- **Unjust persecution.** In today's terms, King Saul was hating on him for no reason at all.
- **Homelessness.** As King Saul was hunting him down to take his life, David had to flee by staying on the move, so he was sleeping at different people's houses every night.
- **Desperation.** With nowhere to turn for help, David actually went to the Philistines, his enemies, for refuge. "Hello," David and Goliath! Goliath was a Philistine.
- **Mental health.** When the Philistines discovered David was among them, he pretended to be mentally ill, which worked, because they let him go.

Now in spite of all this, let's see how David's response helped him, and can also help you and me as we overcome anxiety. First, he praised God. Yep, you heard me right. As his haters were pursuing him, David took the time to praise God. He said, "I bless God every chance I get, my lungs expand with His praise" (Psalm 34:1 MSG). Next, this dude had the audacity to begin to brag on God and his confidence in God's power to change his circumstances before his circumstances actually changed! If that was not bold enough, he turned into a recruiter and was encouraging others to follow his lead, which is exactly what we should do as we deal with the anxieties of life. I implore[27] you to take heed to David's actions so you, too, can experience the fact that the power found in the word of God is still as relevant, life-changing, and life-directing as the day it was written.

---

27 Beg someone earnestly or desperately to do something.

LET'S TALK ABOUT IT

1. In order to properly deal with anxiety, we must first have the ability to identify it. What are some things that are causing, or have caused, you anxiety?
2. What steps or coping mechanisms are you using, or have used in the past, to alleviate anxiety?
3. Are these steps or coping mechanisms in alignment with the word of God?

GO TELL THAT

2 Corinthians 12:10 (NIV)

That is why, for Christ's sake, I delight in weaknesses, in insults, in hardships, in persecutions, in difficulties. For when I am weak, then I am strong.

Psalm 34:1-22 (MSG)

I bless GOD every chance I get;
my lungs expand with his praise.
I live and breathe GOD;
if things aren't going well, hear this and be happy:
Join me in spreading the news;
together let's get the word out.
GOD met me more than halfway,
he freed me from my anxious fears.
Look at him; give him your warmest smile.
Never hide your feelings from him.
When I was desperate, I called out,
and GOD got me out of a tight spot.

GOD's angel sets up a circle
of protection around us while we pray.
Open your mouth and taste, open your eyes and see—
how good GOD is.
Blessed are you who run to him.
Worship GOD if you want the best;
worship opens doors to all his goodness.
Young lions on the prowl get hungry,
but GOD-seekers are full of God.
Come, children, listen closely;
I'll give you a lesson in GOD worship.
Who out there has a lust for life?
Can't wait each day to come upon beauty?
Guard your tongue from profanity,
and no more lying through your teeth.
Turn your back on sin; do something good.
Embrace peace—don't let it get away!
GOD keeps an eye on his friends,
his ears pick up every moan and groan.
GOD won't put up with rebels;
he'll cull them from the pack.
Is anyone crying for help? GOD is listening,
ready to rescue you.
If your heart is broken, you'll find GOD right there;
if you're kicked in the gut, he'll help you catch your breath.
Disciples so often get into trouble;
still, GOD is there every time.
He's your bodyguard, shielding every bone;
not even a finger gets broken.

The wicked commit slow suicide;
they waste their lives hating the good.
GOD pays for each slave's freedom;
no one who runs to him loses out.

DAY 5
CONTENT, NOT COMPLACENT

*I am not saying this because I am in need, for I have learned to
be content whatever the circumstances. I know what it is to be
in need, and I know what it is to have plenty. I have learned the
secret of being content in any and every situation, whether well
fed or hungry, whether living in plenty or in want. I can do all this
through him who gives me strength.*
Philippians 4:11-13 (NIV)

Being content is having a clear understanding that where we pres-
ently are is exactly where God wants us to be because He has work for
us to do. Sometimes we get confused in our thinking that free choice
means we are free to do as we choose. We must never lose sight of
the fact that God created each of us on purpose and *for* His purpose.
However, in order for us to know His purpose for our lives, we must
seek Him for guidance to not only order our steps in regard to where
He would have us to go, but to also have the courage to go where He
leads. Now, let me caution you that once you decide to surrender your
life to Christ and allow Him to be both Lord and Savior, expect adversity to show up stronger than ever.

Our response should be to prepare a plan in advance to overcome the adversity we will encounter as we live a life on assignment
for Christ. This is important because when we expect something to
happen, when it does occur, we are not caught off guard. For instance,
if we knew someone was going to physically attack us, we would not
just sit by idly and wait for it to happen. Instead, we would have our

guard up, and at the same time, while we would be anticipating when, where, and how this attack could happen, we would also be developing a strategy of how to respond. Likewise, when adversity strikes, if we are prepared to overcome it, when it does, we simply rely on our plan and preparation to get us through it, which transforms our adversity from a test to a testimony.

However, as the old adage goes, "Be careful what you ask for." We, too, must understand that there is power in our tongues, and that when we ask God for something in prayer, if it is according to His will, it will come to fruition. Interestingly enough, we pray and ask for promotions and increase, and when God allows them to happen, most of us allow them to go from being blessings to burdens simply because we lose sight of whom we are working to please. Ephesians 6:7 makes it very clear that we are to "work with enthusiasm, as though you were working for the Lord rather than for people" (NLT).

So, that means that as God's children, when He gives us an assignment, we do not second guess ourselves or, most importantly, second guess God at the first sign of adversity—In particular, the adversity of the unknowns we encounter during our difficult seasons. Far too many times we put the proverbial cart in front of the horse when it comes to carrying out our assignments for Christ. In other words, our willingness to totally embrace our assignments becomes contingent upon us knowing the end result either before or while we are executing our assignment. The word "assignment" in and of itself is temporal in nature. In fact, an assignment is something given to us by someone in authority to be completed in a certain amount of time for a particular purpose. Now, because we have free will, we can choose to accept our God-appointed assignments, or we can waste endless amounts of time and energy trying to avoid them, but we must understand there are ramifications that come from disobedience.

This reality leads us to an inevitable fork in the road where we can either choose to allow unfamiliarity to turn our God-ordained assignments down, or to transition us to grow into being all God has called us to be. Let's choose to accept all of our temporary assignments, which will have eternal implications, by being content with where God currently has us, but never complacent because of the fight that lies ahead.

LET'S TALK ABOUT IT

1. Think back over your life in regard to all the many "firsts" you have encountered. How did you deal with the uncertainty of the unknowns?

2. Are these coping mechanisms in step with God's word?

3. Be careful of what you pray for because you might just get it. In fact, if it is according to God's will, then you *will* get it. How does knowing that each temporary assignment has eternal ramifications change how you go about doing what you do?

GO TELL THAT

2 Timothy 4:7 (NLT)

I have fought the good fight, I have finished the race, and I have remained faithful.

Proverbs 18:21 (NLT)

The tongue can bring death or life; those who love to talk will reap the consequences.

Proverbs 18:21 (MSG)

Words kill, words give life;
   they're either poison or fruit—you choose.

2 Corinthians 4:18 (NLT)

So we don't look at the troubles we can see now; rather, we fix our gaze on things that cannot be seen. For the things we see now will soon be gone, but the things we cannot see will last forever.

DAY 4
CALLED TO LIVE A
COUNTERCULTURAL LIFE

Don't copy the behavior and customs of this world, but let God
transform you into a new person by changing the way you think.
Then you will learn to know God's will for you, which is good and
pleasing and perfect.
Romans 12:2 (NLT)

I challenge you to turn on your television or search the internet and you will see countless examples of our current culture aggressively attempting to redefine new norms, such as same-sex marriage or relationships, transgender issues, and abortion. Even the rainbow, which was intended by God to be a symbol to remind us of His covenant, has been used as the symbol for the LGBT community. While I love all my brothers and sisters in Christ, one thing we cannot do as Christians is blend in or condone what is happening. In fact, the Bible has called us to stick out and be bold enough to live a countercultural life.[28] I know what you are thinking: "What exactly does that mean?"

Living a countercultural life means that we choose to live contrary to the world's standards by living in harmony with God's standards as revealed to us in scripture. It means that instead of changing what we believe in daily, weekly, or whenever cultural fads deem necessary, we stay rooted and grounded in the unchanging word of God. It means we stand firm in our convictions while showing the

---

28 Don't copy the behavior and customs of this world, but let God transform you into a new person by changing the way you think. Then you will learn to know God's will for you, which is good and pleasing and perfect. (Romans 12:2 NLT)

love of Christ by how we treat our brothers and sisters in Christ, especially those who have different beliefs than we have. It means we use scripture to correct, rebuke, and teach. So, now I know you are really curious to what that looks like within the flow of everyday life.

First, in order to minister to anyone else, we must first minister to ourselves. We accomplish this by being engaged in a relationship with our heavenly Father, through which we can seek Him for guidance, talk to Him through prayer, and take heed to the actions He places on our hearts in response to His will being done in our lives. This kind of relationship changes us from the inside out, so that we can be a positive, godly influence on everyone we come in contact with. Next, it means we surrender what we want in exchange for being on a mission with Christ to win lives for the kingdom of God. So, every day that God wakes us up, we understand that it is on purpose because we still have purpose. That purpose is to live all 1,440 minutes of each day that God so graciously gives us sold out for Christ. As a result, we invest our time in eternal matters as opposed to wasting it on the fleeting things of this world.[29] Finally, we love like nobody's business. In fact, we love like Christ, with agape love[30].

A Little Deeper

Civil disobedience is the active, professed refusal of a citizen to obey certain laws, demands, orders or commands of a government.[31] While the Bible is very clear that Christians are to obey civil governments as a general rule, if that government ever commands us to do

---

29 So we don't look at the troubles we can see now; rather, we fix our gaze on things that cannot be seen. For the things we see now will soon be gone, but the things we cannot see will last forever. (2 Corinthians 4:18 NLT)

30 Totally unselfish love that comes from God alone. The type of love that chooses to continue selflessly loving someone, even when he or she makes it difficult. Christ's sacrifice and His love model what it means to choose to love.

31 Thoreau 1849

something that violates God's law or forbids us from doing something that God commands, we are to obey God rather than man.[32] Because our government is passing laws that recognize same-sex marriages and transgender rights, and trying to redefine what the home is supposed to look like, living a countercultural life becomes a form of civil disobedience. However, as we practice it, we are to do so not with malice or strife, but as the picture of grace and humility.[33] Although we are obeying God rather than man, we are supposed to be godly men and women who greatly reflect the spirit of Christ as we do so.[34] Let's have the courage to do what is right and not what is popular.

LET'S TALK ABOUT IT

1. Living a countercultural life means to go against the grain or to be different. In what ways do you pride yourself on being different?

2. Are these areas in which you are different in alignment with who you are as a child of God?

3. There is a quote that says, "Just because everyone is doing it does not make it right." That means popularity does not justify doing things that are wrong. Identify some areas that you can have a positive, godly influence by simply having the courage to do what is right as opposed to what is popular.

---

32 Jeremiah 2013
33 ibid.
34 ibid.

GO TELL THAT

James 4:4 (NLT)

You adulterers! Don't you realize that friendship with the world makes you an enemy of God? I say it again: If you want to be a friend of the world, you make yourself an enemy of God.

Colossians 2:7 (NLT)

Let your roots grow down into him, and let your lives be built on him. Then your faith will grow strong in the truth you were taught, and you will overflow with thankfulness.

2 Timothy 4:2 (NLT)

Preach the word of God. Be prepared, whether the time is favorable or not. Patiently correct, rebuke, and encourage your people with good teaching.

DAY 3
BE MINDFUL OF THE COMPANY YOU KEEP

As iron sharpens iron, so one person sharpens another.
Proverbs 27:17 (NIV)

Do any of these statements sound familiar to you?

1. Watch the company you keep.
2. Birds of a feather flock together.
3. Guilty by association.

For as long as you can remember, well-meaning people (family, friends, coaches, etc.) have been advising you to be mindful of the people you surround yourself with for the fear that although you may not be looking for it, trouble may find you due to who you choose to associate with. Another reason is to protect your reputation. Once you get a bad name, that's hard to shake, right? Below is a short list of attributes that, as you read over them, I want you to imagine what it would feel like to have any of them associated with who you are as a person.

- Lazy
- Unreliable
- Untrustworthy
- Uncommitted
- Unmotivated
- Uninvolved
- Uninspired
- Ungrateful
- Unexcited

- Detached
- Weak

Weak? That last one makes me want to fight right now. Weak?! Now let's unpack one of the favorite similes found in the Bible: Proverbs 27:17,

"As iron sharpens iron, so one person sharpens another" (NIV).

The simile contains two interpretations of iron. The first one is iron in its physical state. In the physical state, iron provides great strength, hardness, and determination. As children of God striving to live as holy as a sinner saved by grace can live, that means we get to accept the challenge to undergo the transformation required to become iron. We become iron by making a choice to totally surrender to God's will by obediently following His word, which molds and shapes us into the men and women God has called us to be. Culture will try to make you think this is a bad thing, but in reality, this provides us with relief because we finally get to drop all the facades. Instead of continuing to waste enormous amounts of time pretending to be something we are not for the sake of protecting our reputations, we become free to invest that same time into our relationship with Christ, which allows us to develop our spiritual character. In regard to which is more important, reputation or character, here is what the writer Thomas Paine had to say: "Reputation is what men and women think of us; character is what God and angels know of us." My man, Tim Tebow, in his book, *Shaken,* says, "What God knows about us is more important than what others think about us."[35] Here is what God knows about you and me. Ephesians 2:10 says, "For we are his workmanship, created in Christ Jesus for good works, which God prepared

---

35 Tebow and Gregory 2016

beforehand, that we should walk in them" (NKJV). So, let's walk in who God knows us to be. Let's become iron—Christians with great strength as a result of our faith, hard in regard to our convictions, and determined to live sold out for Christ.

The second interpretation of iron presents another challenge that we get the privilege to accept. Once we become iron, we can now begin to build up our fellow brothers and sisters in Christ. Iron, in this sense, is something that is useful in construction. It is used to build. For us, both you and me, this is the 66 book love letter that God left us. The Bible becomes both our tool for building as well as the grinding block that we sharpen each other on by knowing it, so we can lovingly hold each other to His standards and not the world's.

"As iron sharpens iron, so one person sharpens another" (NIV)

"One person" speaks to the personal responsibilities we each have to one another as godly men and women. In the book, *Raising a Modern-Day Knight*, after the author defines what a godly man is, he immediately goes on to list the responsibilities of a godly man, the first being a will to obey as revealed in the scripture.[36] 1 Thessalonians 5:11 says, "Therefore encourage one another and build each other up..." (NIV). In addition, when Jesus was being questioned in the Bible about which commandment was the greatest, His answer was in alignment with our responsibility to our fellow brothers and sisters.

> "Jesus said unto him, Thou shalt love the Lord thy God with all thy heart, and with all thy soul, and with all thy mind. This is the first and great commandment. And the second is like unto it, Thou shalt love thy neighbour as thyself. On these two commandments hang all the law and the prophets" (Matthew 22:37-39 KJV).

---

36 Lewis 2007

It is that simple. If God said it, then that settles it, so own up to your responsibilities as a godly man or woman and take care of others. Now I'm going to repeat that same short list of attributes from before:

- Lazy
- Unreliable
- Untrustworthy
- Uncommitted
- Unmotivated
- Uninvolved
- Uninspired
- Ungrateful
- Unexcited
- Detached
- Weak

I want you to consider what it would feel like to have any of them associated with you in regard to your character, as the man or woman of God you've been called to be. Since I'm pretty certain that none of us are fond of any of these attributes being attached to us, that means we understand that it is an honor, a privilege, and our responsibility to be active participants in the advancement of the kingdom of God. What can be more awesome than that? I'll tell you what. The fact that we can do it *now*! In the kingdom of God, there is no thirty day grace period that we must wait. We can choose right now, today, through our actions, that reaching the lost is a lifestyle, and sharpening others is a condition of our hearts.

As iron sharpens iron, so one person sharpens another.

So, I ask, who are you sharpening? My prayer is that it will be so many people that you lose count!

LET'S TALK ABOUT IT

1. Who are the people in your life that took the time to sharpen you?

2. In the spirit of paying it forward, who are you currently sharpening?

3. Imagine a world where people take their responsibility to help build up one another as seriously as they cheer for their favorite sports team. Since our thoughts precede our actions, I challenge you to move beyond simply thinking of a world that looks like this and to begin to take the necessary actions to build others up every chance you get. What is the first step for you?

GO TELL THAT

Proverbs 13:20 (MSG)

Become wise by walking with the wise;

    hang out with fools and watch your life fall to pieces.

1 Corinthians 15:33 (NIV)

Do not be misled: "Bad company corrupts good character."

Proverbs 14:7 (MSG)

Escape quickly from the company of fools;

    they're a waste of your time, a waste of your words.

Proverbs 28:7 (NLT)

Young people who obey the law are wise;

    those with wild friends bring shame to their parents.

DAY 2
AN UNEXPECTED END

What, then, shall we say in response to these things? If God is for us, who can be against us? He who did not spare his own Son, but gave him up for us all—how will he not also, along with him, graciously give us all things? Who will bring any charge against those whom God has chosen? It is God who justifies. Who then is the one who condemns? No one. Christ Jesus who died—more than that, who was raised to life—is at the right hand of God and is also interceding for us. Who shall separate us from the love of Christ? Shall trouble or hardship or persecution or famine or nakedness or danger or sword? As it is written:

"For your sake we face death all day long;
we are considered as sheep to be slaughtered." No, in all these things we are more than conquerors through him who loved us. For I am convinced that neither death nor life, neither angels nor demons, neither the present nor the future, nor any powers, neither height nor depth, nor anything else in all creation, will be able to separate us from the love of God that is in Christ Jesus our Lord.
Romans 8:31-39 (NIV)

I can barely type because I am so excited to discuss our expected end as children of God. In addition to our text, the lyrics from Jekalyn Carr's song, "You Will Win," just keep running through my mind over and over, especially when she says, "Everything attached to me wins."[37] If that doesn't get you fired up, I don't know what will! Like, we win! We win! The good guys and ladies, win! So, I hope by this point you

---

37 Carr 2017

are not asking, "Who are the 'we' that I am referring to?" However, just in case you are wondering who "we" is comprised of, I'll gladly explain who we are.

We are God's children, adopted through the shedding of blood, which Jesus did when He died on the cross for all our sins.

"But when the set time had fully come, God sent his Son, born of a woman, born under the law, to redeem those under the law, that we might receive adoption to sonship" (Galatians 4:4-5 NIV).

We are heirs to a heavenly kingdom, along with Jesus, who intercedes for us before God, our Father.

"Now if we are children, then we are heirs—heirs of God and co-heirs with Christ, if indeed we share in his sufferings in order that we may also share in his glory" (Romans 8:17 NIV).

We are those who choose long suffering[38] as a lifestyle as opposed to it being an inconvenience.

"However, for this reason I obtained mercy, that in me first Jesus Christ might show all long suffering, as a pattern to those who are going to believe on Him for everlasting life" (1 Timothy 1:16 NKJV).

We are overcomers of sickness, diseases, job loss, financial hardships, global pandemics, and any other curve balls life tries to throw at us, because nothing can get us to stop trusting in God.

"Do not be anxious about anything, but in every situation, by prayer and petition, with thanksgiving, present your requests to God. And the peace of God, which transcends all understanding, will guard your hearts and your minds in Christ Jesus" (Philippians 4:6-7 NIV).

---

38 The quiet willingness to accept both painful and irritating situations.

We are those who pray and praise in spite of our haters because our God is so good.

"Taste and see that the LORD is good;
blessed is the one who takes refuge in him" (Psalm 34:8 NIV).

We *are* those who choose to walk by faith and not by sight because we understand that seeing is not believing to a child of God. Faith for us is believing and seeing things as they are to be, *not* as they are.

"Now faith is confidence in what we hope for and assurance about what we do not see" (Hebrews 11:1 NIV).

We are those who willingly choose to lose our lives in regard to the world's standards so that we may find life, both now and eternally, in the presence of the Lord.

"Whoever finds their life will lose it, and whoever loses their life for my sake will find it" (Matthew 10:39 NIV).

We are more than conquerors. We are victors who do not fight *for* victory, but instead fight *from* victory because once we have accepted Jesus as our Lord and Savior, victory is already ours!

"But thanks be to God! He gives us the victory through our Lord Jesus Christ" (1 Corinthians 15:57 NIV).

"For everyone born of God overcomes the world. This is the victory that has overcome the world, even our faith. Who is it that overcomes the world? Only the one who believes that Jesus is the Son of God" (1 John 5:4-5 NIV).

So, this is who *we* are. But now the narrative turns to who are *you* right now at this point in your life, and will you choose to join us? We have covered a wide range of topics in this devotional, but none are as important as this. At some point, we must all make a decision to either accept Jesus as our Lord and Savior or live apart from Him as His adversary. Philippians 2:10-11 is very clear when it says, "that at the name of Jesus every knee should bow, of those in heaven, and of those on earth, and of those under the earth, and that every tongue should confess that Jesus Christ is Lord, to the glory of God the Father" (NKJV). My prayer is that today, right now, while you have this devotional open, that you will respond to one of the three appeals I am getting ready to make. My first appeal is that if you have never accepted Jesus as your Lord and Savior, that you would welcome Him in your heart by reciting the following prayer, affectionately known as the sinner's prayer. *(The prayer is listed at the end of this message, so if this is you, stop reading and go recite it now.)* My second appeal is to those of us who have accepted Jesus before and may have even been baptized, but have wandered away from the faith—that you would make a decision to come back home. The easiest thing to do is connect with a family member, friend, co-worker, or associate you know who is currently living out loud and on fire for Christ. They will be thrilled to help you reconnect with a local church as well as help guide you on your journey to grow spiritually. My last appeal is to those who are already on the front lines fighting the good fight of faith for Christ—that we all be determined to do even more. So, every morning God wakes us up, we understand that it is because we still have purpose. That purpose is to take that 1,440 minutes that He has so graciously given us, and to be intentional about winning lives for Him by being determined to continue running by faith.

LET'S TALK ABOUT IT

1. Who is Jesus Christ to you?
2. Do you believe there is a Heaven and a hell? Why or why not?
3. If you were to die today, where would you spend eternity?

GO TELL THAT

Romans 3:23 (NIV)

For all have sinned and fall short of the glory of God.

Romans 6:23 (NIV)

For the wages of sin is death, but the gift of God is eternal life in Christ Jesus our Lord.

John 3:3 (NIV)

Jesus replied, "Very truly I tell you, no one can see the kingdom of God unless they are born again."

Revelation 3:20 (NLT)

"Look! I stand at the door and knock. If you hear my voice and open the door, I will come in, and we will share a meal together as friends."

THE SINNER'S PRAYER

Dear God in Heaven, I come to You in the name of Jesus. I acknowledge to You that I am a sinner, and I am sorry for the sins and the life that I have lived; I need Your forgiveness. I believe that Your only begotten Son, Jesus Christ, shed His precious blood on the cross at Calvary and died for my sins, and I am now willing to turn from my sin. You said in Your Holy Word, Romans 10:9, that if we confess the Lord our God and believe in our hearts that God raised Jesus from the dead, we shall be saved. Right now, I confess Jesus as the Lord of my soul. With my heart, I believe that God raised Jesus from the dead. This very moment, I accept Jesus Christ as my own personal Savior and according to His word, right now, I am saved. Thank You, Jesus, for Your unlimited grace which has saved me from my sins. I thank You, Jesus, that Your grace never leads to license, but rather it always leads to repentance. Therefore, Lord Jesus, transform my life so that I may bring glory and honor to You alone and not to myself. Thank You, Jesus, for dying for me and giving me eternal life.

Amen.

DAY 1
THE BEGINNING

Therefore, if anyone is in Christ, the new creation has come:
The old has gone, the new is here!
2 Corinthians 5:17 (NIV)

Today is the beginning of the rest of your life as either a new believer in Christ Jesus or as a rededicated, reenergized vessel of hope that God can use to reach others. Your past failures are exactly that, a thing of the past, and no matter what may be back there, God is already using your past to qualify you for the calling that is now in front of you. I pray you will boldly embrace your identity in Christ, which, since He created you, is your *true* identity, and not who the world has constantly tried to tell you who you are. Have faith that you are more than good enough because you are. God created you on purpose, and with a purpose, to live your life on assignment for His will to be done. Go be intentional to lead by following God as you *run by faith* today and every day that God wakes you up. You got this because God has got you covered by the blood of His One and Only Son, Jesus Christ!

LET'S TALK ABOUT IT

1. When we enjoy a good experience, such as a good meal at a restaurant, we can't wait to tell everyone we know about it. In essence, we share our testimony about our experience. Who

can benefit from you sharing your testimony when it comes to what God has done for you, so they, too, can run by faith?

2. Running by faith for Christ cannot be done by playing it safe on the sidelines. It takes getting out of our comfort zones, getting into the game, and then trusting God to guide us to be beacons of light to lead others to Him. What obstacles will you have to overcome to share your faith with others?

3. The world tries to remind us of our past failures to discourage us, but God uses our past failures to qualify us for the calling He has on our lives. How can you allow God to use your past setbacks to become areas of ministry?

GO TELL THAT

2 Corinthians 5:15 (NIV)

And he died for all, that those who live should no longer live for themselves but for him who died for them and was raised again.

Romans 10:9-11 (NLT)

If you openly declare that Jesus is Lord and believe in your heart that God raised him from the dead, you will be saved. For it is by believing in your heart that you are made right with God, and it is by openly declaring your faith that you are saved. As the Scriptures tell us, "Anyone who trusts in him will never be disgraced."

FROM THE AUTHOR

I want to set the record straight that this book has nothing, I mean absolutely nothing, to do with me, and everything to do with honoring my Lord and Savior Jesus Christ. I am not that important or significant besides my willingness to be a vessel through which He has chosen to carry His message to His people. I was born and raised in the South, where there are two things that are woven into the fabric of our DNA: church and sports. As a child, my parents instilled in me and my siblings the importance of having a relationship with God. Although I always attended church on a regular basis, it was not until my second season in the National Football League that I stopped playing church and made the decision to die to my own selfish will so that I could be available to be used for God's good and perfect will. That was over twenty years ago, and in addition to the many wonderful things Christ has been able to do through me for His glory, *Running by Faith* is another example of how God can use the unqualified to do the unlikely as long as it is in His will. It has been an absolute honor to grow closer to God through this endeavor, and my prayer is that I will continue to be obedient to Christ to the point where instead of being known by my name, Autry L Denson, Jr., people will come to simply know me as a child of God.

ABOUT THIS BOOK

There is a quote that says, "If you are too busy to take the time out to pray or read the Bible, then you are far busier than God ever intended for you to be." We live in a world where there are so many things competing for our time. In fact, we have smart phones, smart houses, and all types of gadgets that are designed to make our lives simple and keep us connected to one another, but in reality, have led to us being more disconnected than ever. So, in the essence of being respectful of your time, *Running by Faith* includes twenty-three short, simple messages based on the inerrant word of God, designed as what an appetizer is to a full course meal. I want to ignite your appetite for Christ, to the point where you move past just wanting to spend more time hanging out with God in prayer and reading the Bible, to not only doing it, but enjoying it because you feel and see the personal growth. As a result of your own personal growth, you will then feel both empowered and emphatic about helping as many people as you can to seek out a personal relationship with Christ where they can turn around and disciple others. It is imperative that we open our mouths and operate with a sense of urgency that this life-and-death situation requires, so that no one will perish without having the opportunity to accept Jesus as their Lord and Savior. I urge and pray that after reading this book, you will be compelled to run by faith, and tell everyone you can about what God has done for you, and what He can do for them.

BIBLE VERSE INDEX

DAY 23—YOUR WORD IS YOUR BOND

Matthew 5:33-37 (MSG)

"And don't say anything you don't mean. This counsel is embedded deep in our traditions. You only make things worse when you lay down a smoke screen of pious talk, saying, 'I'll pray for you,' and never doing it, or saying, 'God be with you,' and not meaning it. You don't make your words true by embellishing them with religious lace. In making your speech sound more religious, it becomes less true. Just say 'yes' and 'no.' When you manipulate words to get your own way, you go wrong."

DAY 22—WARNING!

1 Peter 3:18 (NIV)

For Christ also suffered once for sins, the righteous for the unrighteous, to bring you to God. He was put to death in the body but made alive in the Spirit.

Romans 10:17 (NIV)

Consequently, faith comes from hearing the message, and the message is heard through the word about Christ.

Hebrews 10:25 (NIV)

Not giving up meeting together, as some are in the habit of doing, but encouraging one another—and all the more as you see the Day approaching.

1 Timothy 4:16 (NIV)

Watch your life and doctrine closely. Persevere in them, because if you do, you will save both yourself and your hearers.

DAY 21—THE GOOD LIFE

2 Corinthians 4:18 (NIV)

So we fix our eyes not on what is seen, but on what is unseen, since what is seen is temporary, but what is unseen is eternal.

Matthew 22:36-40 (NIV)

"Teacher, which is the greatest commandment in the Law?"

Jesus replied: "'Love the Lord your God with all your heart and with all your soul and with all your mind.' This is the first and greatest commandment. And the second is like it: 'Love your neighbor as yourself.' All the Law and the Prophets hang on these two commandments."

Matthew 28:16-20 (NIV)

Then the eleven disciples went to Galilee, to the mountain where Jesus had told them to go. When they saw him, they worshiped him; but some doubted. Then Jesus came to them and said, "All authority in heaven and on earth has been given to me. Therefore go and make disciples of all nations, baptizing them in the name of the Father and of the Son and of the Holy Spirit, and teaching them to obey everything I have commanded you. And surely I am with you always, to the very end of the age."

DAY 20—THE GOLDEN RULE

Luke 6:31 (ESV)

And as you wish that others would do to you, do so to them.

Mark 12:31 (ESV)

"The second is this: 'You shall love your neighbor as yourself.' There is no other commandment greater than these."

DAY 19—THE DEAL OF A LIFETIME: FAITHFUL TITHING

Genesis 14:19-20 (NIV)

> And he blessed Abram, saying,
>
> "Blessed be Abram by God Most High,
>
> Creator of heaven and earth.
>
> And praise be to God Most High,
>
> who delivered your enemies into your hand."
>
> Then Abram gave him a tenth of everything.

Deuteronomy 12:5-6 (NIV)

> But you are to seek the place the LORD your God will choose from among all your tribes to put his Name there for his dwelling. To that place you must go; there bring your burnt offerings and sacrifices, your tithes and special gifts, what you have vowed to give and your freewill offerings, and the firstborn of your herds and flocks.

DAY 18—RESET

Luke 23:34 (NIV)

> Jesus said, "Father, forgive them, for they do not know what they are doing." And they divided up his clothes by casting lots.

Ephesians 4:32 (NIV)

> Be kind and compassionate to one another, forgiving each other, just as in Christ God forgave you.

Hebrews 12:14 (NIV)

> Make every effort to live in peace with everyone and to be holy; without holiness no one will see the Lord.

Romans 5:10 (NIV)

For if, while we were God's enemies, we were reconciled to him through the death of his Son, how much more, having been reconciled, shall we be saved through his life!

DAY 17—RANDOM ACTS OF KINDNESS

1 Corinthians 3:7 (NIV)

So neither the one who plants nor the one who waters is anything, but only God, who makes things grow.

John 3:30 (NIV)

He must become greater; I must become less."

1 Corinthians 10:31 (NIV)

So whether you eat or drink or whatever you do, do it all for the glory of God.

DAY 16—LET'S TALK ABOUT SEX

1 Corinthians 6:12-20 (ESV)

"All things are lawful for me," but not all things are helpful. "All things are lawful for me," but I will not be dominated by anything. "Food is meant for the stomach and the stomach for food"—and God will destroy both one and the other. The body is not meant for sexual immorality, but for the Lord, and the Lord for the body. And God raised the Lord and will also raise us up by his power. Do you not know that your bodies are members of Christ? Shall I then take the members of Christ and make them members of a prostitute? Never! Or do you not know that he who is joined to a prostitute becomes one body with her? For, as it is written, "The two will become one flesh." But he who is joined to the Lord becomes one spirit with him. Flee from sexual immorality. Every other sin a person commits is outside the body, but the sexually immoral person sins against his own body. Or do you not know that your body is a temple of the Holy Spirit within you, whom you have from God? You are not your own, for you were bought with a price. So glorify God in your body.

1 Corinthians 7:1-16 (ESV)

Now concerning the matters about which you wrote: "It is good for a man not to have sexual relations with a woman." But because of the temptation to sexual immorality, each man should have his own wife and each woman her own husband. The husband should give to his wife her conjugal rights, and likewise the wife to her husband. For the wife does not have authority over her own body, but the husband does. Likewise the husband does not have authority over his own body, but the wife does. Do not deprive one another, except perhaps by agreement for a limited time, that you may devote yourselves to prayer; but then come together again, so that Satan may not tempt you because of your lack of self-control.

Now as a concession, not a command, I say this. I wish that all were as I myself am. But each has his own gift from God, one of one kind and one of another.

To the unmarried and the widows I say that it is good for them to remain single, as I am. But if they cannot exercise self-control, they should marry. For it is better to marry than to burn with passion.

To the married I give this charge (not I, but the Lord): the wife should not separate from her husband (but if she does, she should remain unmarried or else be reconciled to her husband), and the husband should not divorce his wife.

To the rest I say (I, not the Lord) that if any brother has a wife who is an unbeliever, and she consents to live with him, he should not divorce her. If any woman has a husband who is an unbeliever, and he consents to live with her, she should not divorce him. For the unbelieving husband is made holy because of his wife, and the unbelieving wife is made holy because of her husband. Otherwise your children would be unclean, but as it is, they are holy. But if the unbelieving partner separates, let it be so. In such cases the brother or sister is not enslaved. God has called you to peace. For how do you know, wife, whether you will save your husband? Or how do you know, husband, whether you will save your wife?

Genesis 2:24 (NLT)

This explains why a man leaves his father and mother and is joined to his wife, and the two are united into one.

Proverbs 5:17-20 (MSG)

Your spring water is for you and you only,
    not to be passed around among strangers.
Bless your fresh-flowing fountain!
    Enjoy the wife you married as a young man!
Lovely as an angel, beautiful as a rose—
    don't ever quit taking delight in her body.
    Never take her love for granted!
Why would you trade enduring intimacies for cheap thrills
    with a whore?
    for dalliance with a promiscuous stranger?

DAY 15—INTOXICATED

Proverbs 20:1 (NIV)

> Wine is a mocker and beer a brawler;
>
> whoever is led astray by them is not wise.

Proverbs 23:31-32 (NIV)

> Do not gaze at wine when it is red,
>
> when it sparkles in the cup,
>
> when it goes down smoothly!
>
> In the end it bites like a snake
>
> and poisons like a viper.

1 Corinthians 5:11 (NIV)

> But now I am writing to you that you must not associate with anyone who claims to be a brother or sister but is sexually immoral or greedy, an idolater or slanderer, a drunkard or swindler. Do not even eat with such people.

Romans 13:13 (NIV)

> Let us behave decently, as in the daytime, not in carousing and drunkenness, not in sexual immorality and debauchery, not in dissension and jealousy.

DAY 14—IN DUE TIME

Psalm 37:7 (KJV)

> Rest in the Lord, and wait patiently for him: fret not thyself because of him who prospereth in his way, because of the man who bringeth wicked devices to pass.

Numbers 23:19 (NLT)

> God is not a man, so he does not lie.
>
> He is not human, so he does not change his mind.

Has he ever spoken and failed to act?

Has he ever promised and not carried it through?

DAY 13—I CHOOSE LOVE

1 Corinthians 11:1 (NLT)

And you should imitate me, just as I imitate Christ.

Isaiah 58:9-12 (MSG)

"If you get rid of unfair practices,

quit blaming victims,

quit gossiping about other people's sins,

If you are generous with the hungry

and start giving yourselves to the down-and-out,

Your lives will begin to glow in the darkness,

your shadowed lives will be bathed in sunlight.

I will always show you where to go.

I'll give you a full life in the emptiest of places—

firm muscles, strong bones.

You'll be like a well-watered garden,

a gurgling spring that never runs dry.

You'll use the old rubble of past lives to build anew,

rebuild the foundations from out of your past.

You'll be known as those who can fix anything,

restore old ruins, rebuild and renovate,

make the community livable again."

Ephesians 2:10 (NIV)

For we are God's handiwork, created in Christ Jesus to do good works, which God prepared in advance for us to do.

DAY 12—EVERYDAY HEROES OF FAITH

Hebrews 11:1-40 (NLT)

Faith shows the reality of what we hope for; it is the evidence of things we cannot see. Through their faith, the people in days of old earned a good reputation.

By faith we understand that the entire universe was formed at God's command, that what we now see did not come from anything that can be seen.

It was by faith that Abel brought a more acceptable offering to God than Cain did. Abel's offering gave evidence that he was a righteous man, and God showed his approval of his gifts. Although Abel is long dead, he still speaks to us by his example of faith.

It was by faith that Enoch was taken up to heaven without dying—"he disappeared, because God took him." For before he was taken up, he was known as a person who pleased God. And it is impossible to please God without faith. Anyone who wants to come to him must believe that God exists and that he rewards those who sincerely seek him.

It was by faith that Noah built a large boat to save his family from the flood. He obeyed God, who warned him about things that had never happened before. By his faith Noah condemned the rest of the world, and he received the righteousness that comes by faith.

It was by faith that Abraham obeyed when God called him to leave home and go to another land that God would give him as his inheritance. He went without knowing where he was going. And even when he reached the land God promised him, he lived there by faith—for he was like a foreigner, living in tents. And so did Isaac and Jacob, who inherited the same promise. Abraham was confidently looking forward to a city with eternal foundations, a city designed and built by God.

It was by faith that even Sarah was able to have a child, though she was barren and was too old. She believed that God would keep his promise. And so a whole nation came from this one man who was as good as dead—a nation with so many people that, like the stars in the sky and the sand on the seashore, there is no way to count them.

All these people died still believing what God had promised them. They did not receive what was promised, but they saw it all from a distance and welcomed it. They agreed that they were foreigners and nomads here on earth. Obviously people who say such things are looking forward to a country they can call their own. If they had longed for the country they came from, they could have gone back. But they were looking for a better place, a heavenly homeland. That is why God is not ashamed to be called their God, for he has prepared a city for them.

It was by faith that Abraham offered Isaac as a sacrifice when God was testing him. Abraham, who had received God's promises, was ready to sacrifice his only son, Isaac, even though God had told him, "Isaac is the son through whom your descendants will be counted." Abraham reasoned that if Isaac died, God was able to bring him back to life again. And in a sense, Abraham did receive his son back from the dead.

It was by faith that Isaac promised blessings for the future to his sons, Jacob and Esau.

It was by faith that Jacob, when he was old and dying, blessed each of Joseph's sons and bowed in worship as he leaned on his staff.

It was by faith that Joseph, when he was about to die, said confidently that the people of Israel would leave Egypt. He even commanded them to take his bones with them when they left.

It was by faith that Moses' parents hid him for three months when he was born. They saw that God had given them an unusual child, and they were not afraid to disobey the king's command.

It was by faith that Moses, when he grew up, refused to be called the son of Pharaoh's daughter. He chose to share the oppression of God's people instead of enjoying the fleeting pleasures of sin. He thought it was better to suffer for the sake of Christ than to own the treasures of Egypt, for he was looking ahead to his great reward. It was by faith that Moses left the land of Egypt, not fearing the king's anger. He kept right on going because he kept his eyes on the one who is invisible. It was by faith that Moses commanded the people of Israel to keep the Passover and to sprinkle blood on the doorposts so that the angel of death would not kill their firstborn sons.

It was by faith that the people of Israel went right through the Red Sea as though they were on dry ground. But when the Egyptians tried to follow, they were all drowned.

It was by faith that the people of Israel marched around Jericho for seven days, and the walls came crashing down.

It was by faith that Rahab the prostitute was not destroyed with the people in her city who refused to obey God. For she had given a friendly welcome to the spies.

How much more do I need to say? It would take too long to recount the stories of the faith of Gideon, Barak, Samson, Jephthah, David, Samuel, and all the prophets. By faith these people overthrew kingdoms, ruled with justice, and received what God had promised them. They shut the mouths of lions, quenched the flames of fire, and escaped death by the edge of the sword. Their weakness was turned to strength. They became strong in battle and put whole armies to flight. Women received their loved ones back again from death.

But others were tortured, refusing to turn from God in order to be set free. They placed their hope in a better life after the resurrection. Some were jeered at, and their backs were cut open with whips. Others were chained in prisons. Some died by stoning, some were sawed in half, and others were killed with the sword. Some went about wearing skins of sheep and goats, destitute and oppressed and mistreated. They were too good for this world, wandering over deserts and mountains, hiding in caves and holes in the ground.

All these people earned a good reputation because of their faith, yet none of them received all that God had promised. For God had something better in mind for us, so that they would not reach perfection without us.

DAY 11—HEADPHONES AND SMARTPHONES: THE CURRENT DOORWAYS TO SECRET SINS

Galatians 6:7 (NLT)

Don't be misled—you cannot mock the justice of God. You will always harvest what you plant.

Matthew 6:22-23 (NLT)

"Your eye is like a lamp that provides light for your body. When your eye is healthy, your whole body is filled with light. But when your eye is unhealthy, your whole body is filled with darkness. And if the light you think you have is actually darkness, how deep that darkness is!"

1 Peter 5:8 (NLT)

Stay alert! Watch out for your great enemy, the devil. He prowls around like a roaring lion, looking for someone to devour.

DAY 10—GREATNESS: GHEA – GOD HONORING EFFORT AND ATTITUDE

Ephesians 6:7-8 (NIV)

Serve wholeheartedly, as if you were serving the Lord, not people, because you know that the Lord will reward each one for whatever good they do, whether they are slave or free.

Colossians 3:23 (NIV)

Whatever you do, work at it with all your heart, as working for the Lord, not for human masters.

Ecclesiastes 5:18-20 (NIV)

This is what I have observed to be good: that it is appropriate for a person to eat, to drink and to find satisfaction in their toilsome labor under the sun during the few days of life God has given them—for this is their lot. Moreover, when God gives someone wealth and possessions, and the ability to enjoy them, to accept their lot and be happy in their toil—this is a gift of God. They seldom reflect on the days of their life, because God keeps them occupied with gladness of heart.

DAY 9—FOR THE LOVE OF MONEY

Matthew 19:23 (NIV)

Then Jesus said to his disciples, "Truly I tell you, it is hard for someone who is rich to enter the kingdom of heaven."

Matthew 6:24 (NIV)

"No one can serve two masters. Either you will hate the one and love the other, or you will be devoted to the one and despise the other. You cannot serve both God and money."

DAY 8—DISTRACTIONS

Ephesians 5:31 (MSG)

And this is why a man leaves father and mother and cherishes his wife. No longer two, they become "one flesh."

1 Corinthians 7:8-9 (ESV)

To the unmarried and the widows I say that it is good for them to remain single, as I am. But if they cannot exercise self-control, they should marry. For it is better to marry than to burn with passion.

1 Thessalonians 4:3-5 (ESV)

For this is the will of God, your sanctification: that you abstain from sexual immorality; that each one of you know how to control his own body in holiness and honor, not in the passion of lust like the Gentiles who do not know God.

John 3:16 (NIV)

For God so loved the world that he gave his one and only Son, that whoever believes in him shall not perish but have eternal life.

Ephesians 2:8 (NLT)

God saved you by his grace when you believed. And you can't take credit for this; it is a gift from God.

DAY 7—DEBT

Psalm 24:1-2 (NIV)

The earth is the LORD's, and everything in it,
the world, and all who live in it;
for he founded it on the seas
and established it on the waters.

Matthew 25:21 (NIV)

"Well done, good and faithful servant! You have been faithful with a few things; I will put you in charge of many things. Come and share your master's happiness!"

Colossians 3:23-24 (NIV)

Whatever you do, work at it with all your heart, as working for the Lord, not for human masters, since you know that you will receive an inheritance from the Lord as a reward. It is the Lord Christ you are serving.

John 10:10 (NLT)

My purpose is to give them a rich and satisfying life.

Galatians 5:1 (NIV)

It is for freedom that Christ has set us free. Stand firm, then, and do not let yourselves be burdened again by a yoke of slavery.

DAY 6—DEALING WITH ANXIETY

2 Corinthians 12:10 (NIV)

That is why, for Christ's sake, I delight in weaknesses, in insults, in hardships, in persecutions, in difficulties. For when I am weak, then I am strong.

Psalm 34:1-22 (MSG)

I bless GOD every chance I get;
my lungs expand with his praise.

I live and breathe GOD;
if things aren't going well, hear this and be happy:

Join me in spreading the news;
together let's get the word out.

GOD met me more than halfway,
he freed me from my anxious fears.

Look at him; give him your warmest smile.
Never hide your feelings from him.

When I was desperate, I called out,
and GOD got me out of a tight spot.

GOD's angel sets up a circle
of protection around us while we pray.

Open your mouth and taste, open your eyes and see—
how good GOD is.

Blessed are you who run to him.

Worship GOD if you want the best;
worship opens doors to all his goodness.

Young lions on the prowl get hungry,
but GOD-seekers are full of God.

Come, children, listen closely;
I'll give you a lesson in GOD worship.

Who out there has a lust for life?
Can't wait each day to come upon beauty?

Guard your tongue from profanity,
and no more lying through your teeth.

Turn your back on sin; do something good.
Embrace peace—don't let it get away!

GOD keeps an eye on his friends,
his ears pick up every moan and groan.

GOD won't put up with rebels;
he'll cull them from the pack.

Is anyone crying for help? GOD is listening,
ready to rescue you.

If your heart is broken, you'll find GOD right there;
if you're kicked in the gut, he'll help you catch your breath.

Disciples so often get into trouble;
still, GOD is there every time.

He's your bodyguard, shielding every bone;
not even a finger gets broken.

The wicked commit slow suicide;
they waste their lives hating the good.

GOD pays for each slave's freedom;
no one who runs to him loses out.

DAY 5—CONTENT, NOT COMPLACENT

2 Timothy 4:7 (NLT)

> I have fought the good fight, I have finished the race, and I have remained faithful.

Proverbs 18:21 (NLT)

> The tongue can bring death or life; those who love to talk will reap the consequences.

Proverbs 18:21 (MSG)

> Words kill, words give life;
>
> > they're either poison or fruit—you choose.

2 Corinthians 4:18 (NLT)

> So we don't look at the troubles we can see now; rather, we fix our gaze on things that cannot be seen. For the things we see now will soon be gone, but the things we cannot see will last forever.

DAY 4—CALLED TO LIVE A COUNTERCULTURAL LIFE

James 4:4 (NLT)

> You adulterers! Don't you realize that friendship with the world makes you an enemy of God? I say it again: If you want to be a friend of the world, you make yourself an enemy of God.

Colossians 2:7 (NLT)

> Let your roots grow down into him, and let your lives be built on him. Then your faith will grow strong in the truth you were taught, and you will overflow with thankfulness.

2 Timothy 4:2 (NLT)

> Preach the word of God. Be prepared, whether the time is favorable or not. Patiently correct, rebuke, and encourage your people with good teaching.

DAY 3—BE MINDFUL OF THE COMPANY YOU KEEP

Proverbs 13:20 (MSG)

> Become wise by walking with the wise;
>> hang out with fools and watch your life fall to pieces.

1 Corinthians 15:33 (NIV)

> Do not be misled: "Bad company corrupts good character."

Proverbs 14:7 (MSG)

> Escape quickly from the company of fools;
>> they're a waste of your time, a waste of your words.

Proverbs 28:7 (NLT)

> Young people who obey the law are wise;
>> those with wild friends bring shame to their parents.

DAY 2—AN UNEXPECTED END

Romans 3:23 (NIV)

> For all have sinned and fall short of the glory of God.

Romans 6:23 (NIV)

> For the wages of sin is death, but the gift of God is eternal life in Christ Jesus our Lord.

John 3:3 (NIV)

> Jesus replied, "Very truly I tell you, no one can see the kingdom of God unless they are born again."

Revelation 3:20 (NLT)

> "Look! I stand at the door and knock. If you hear my voice and open the door, I will come in, and we will share a meal together as friends."

DAY 1—THE BEGINNING

2 Corinthians 5:15 (NIV)

And he died for all, that those who live should no longer live for themselves but for him who died for them and was raised again.

Romans 10:9-11 (NLT)

If you openly declare that Jesus is Lord and believe in your heart that God raised him from the dead, you will be saved. For it is by believing in your heart that you are made right with God, and it is by openly declaring your faith that you are saved. As the Scriptures tell us, "Anyone who trusts in him will never be disgraced."

BIBLIOGRAPHY

Achtemeier, Paul J. *HarperCollins Bible Dictionary*. Place of Publication: HarperOne, 1996.

Carr, Jekalyn. "You Will Win." Track 8 on *One Nation Under God*, Lunjeal Music Group, 2017, compact disc.

Carson, D.A. *Goodreads*. December 2, 2020. https://www.goodreads.com/quotes/99185-people-do-not-drift-toward-holiness-apart-from-grace-driven-effort (accessed December 2, 2020).

Jeremiah, David. *The Jeremiah Study Bible*. Place of Publication: Publisher, Year of Publication.

Lee, Trip, "SONG TITLE." Recorded date (if available). Track Number on *The Good Life*, Reach Records, 2012, compact disc.

Lewis, Robert. *Raising a Modern-Day Knight: A Father's Role in Guiding His Son to Authentic Manhood*. Carol Stream, Illinois: Tyndale House Publishers, 2007.

Merriam-Webster Dictionary, s.v. "greatness" and "love," accessed date, https://www.merriam-webster.com/dictionary/greatness and https://www.merriam-webster.com/dictionary/love.

Salt-N-Pepa, "Let's Talk About Sex." Recorded date (if available). Track 10 on *Blacks' Magic*, The Island Def Jam Music Group, 1990, compact disc.

Tebow, Tim, and A.J. Gregory. *Shaken: Discovering Your True Identity in the Midst of Life's Storms*. New York: WaterBrook, 2016.

Thoreau, Henry David. *Civil Disobedience*. 1849.

Welchel, Hugh. "Four Principles of Biblical Stewardship." November 26, 2012. https://tifwe.org/?s=Four+principles+of+stewardship

ABOUT THE AUTHOR

Autry Lamont Denson (born December 8, 1976) is a Christian author and an American gridiron football coach and former player. He is currently the head football coach at Charleston Southern University, a position he has held since 2019. Denson played college football as a running back at the University of Notre Dame. He played professionally for four seasons in the National Football League (NFL) with the Miami Dolphins, the Indianapolis Colts, and the Chicago Bears and one season in the Canadian Football League (CFL) with the Montreal Alouettes. After retiring from professional sports, Denson spent several years in the financial industry working for New York Life, HomBanc Mortgage Corp., Wachovia, and Merrill Lynch. In 2009, upon accepting his calling to go into ministry, God moved Denson away from the financial industry and back into sports where he mentored young student-athletes in South Florida, through his P.O.I.S.E program, (Perseverance, Opportunity, Intelligence, Sacrifice,

Effort), which promoted spiritual growth, academic development, character training, and sports specific training. A year later, Autry and his wife, Elaine continued to use the platform of athletics to serve the needs of the South Florida community through their Run For Your Goal, NFL Flag Football League, as well as, Autry serving as the head football coach at Pope John Paul II High School in Boca Raton, Florida (2010). After only one season, God transitioned Denson and his family to the college football ranks (2011), where he and his family's outreach ministry would make stops in the following football programs: Bethune-Cookmen University (2011-2013), Miami University (2014) The University of South Florida (2015), and his alma mater the University of Notre Dame (2015-2019). Autry attributes everything in his life to the grace of God, and in spite of the hectic schedule of a college football coach, he was able to attend and graduate from seminary school at Liberty University, where he received his Master of Arts in Christian Leadership (Summer of 2016). He currently lives in Summerville, SC with his wife Elaine of 16 years. He is the father of four children, Ashley, Autry III, Elijah, and Asia and grandfather of twins Ace and Aubrey. Autry sees football as the platform God has so graciously given him to win lives and not just games.

Made in the USA
Las Vegas, NV
02 June 2021

24051309R00075